Advance Praise for *Let the Story Do the Work*

"A well-written and thought-provoking guide on how to create and communicate a persuasive story. Choy demystifies the process of writing and communicating by giving the reader a structure and framework for success."

—Kathi Elster, coauthor of *Working with You Is Killing Me,*
Working for You Isn't Working for Me, and *Mean Girls at Work*

"Trying to get ahead in life without reading this book is like going into a duel unarmed. Esther Choy converts art to virtual science, providing an extraordinary guide to winning with story-telling. It is enjoyable reading and filled with valuable lessons."

—Lloyd E. Shefsky, Retired Clinical Professor, Kellogg School of Management;
consultant to entrepreneurs and family enterprises; author of
Entrepreneurs Are Made Not Born, and Visionaries Are Made Not Born

"In our world of sound bites and information overload, storytelling has the power to persuade, to connect, and to inspire individuals to take action. In *Let the Story Do the Work*, Choy deconstructs the mystery of a great story, and presents compelling, practical techniques to make your message stand out and sink in. It will be required reading for members of my organization to enrich both their presentations and their one-on-one communications."

—Rose Fealy, CFO, major Chicago cultural institution

"In this book Esther Choy gives us a lively lesson in storytelling. *Let the Story Do the Work* gives you the tools to bring your own story to life, and to influence, engage, and inspire with your stories."

—Andreas Kuster, Owner of Jakob's Basler Leckerly,
Switzerland, Founded in 1753

"Esther Choy convinced me to use storytelling in teaching quantitative methods and talking to industry practitioners about big data and other modern data science concepts. While I was skeptical at first, the storytelling worked! Now I regularly use Esther's ideas—clearly laid out in *Let the Story Do the Work*—when I need to talk about difficult technical material. Read this book, try it out, and observe how Esther's approach to storytelling will work wonders for you as well."

—Karl Schmedders, Ph.D., Chair of Quantitative Business Administration,
University of Zurich; Director of Knowledge Transfer, Swiss Finance Institute

"This book debunks the myth that storytellers are born and not made. Esther Choy empowers us with formulas and tools that will make us better storytellers—able to craft impactful 'yarns' that can inspire audiences. Having had the opportunity to test the three-act storytelling process and the various templates in the book, I can say from experience that these concepts make a significant and immediate difference. I wish I had access to this book decades ago."

—Justin Craig, Ph.D., Co-Director, Center for Family Enterprises, Kellogg
School of Management, and coauthor, Leading a Family Enterprise

"Esther Choy shepherded me through an MBA rebirth story—and my admission results at top-tier business schools went from "all denied" to "all accepted"! In doing so, she also gave me storytelling tools that have equipped me for my post-MBA executive quest. She's packed that panoply and more into *Let the Story Do the Work* so you can arm yourself to write your own business success story—among others."

—James Immordino, marketing executive at a major global media company

"It's no secret that stories make facts memorable and relatable. But most people who consider themselves not creative struggle to create narratives that convey facts in a way that engages the listener. *Let the Story Do the Work* offers frameworks for structuring crisp stories that flow and leave the listener with the most important takeaways. This is a powerful, yet accessible book that will motivate and help anyone seeking to excel in the art and science of storytelling."

—Michael F. Malone, Associate Dean, EMBA
and MBA programs, Columbia Business School

"*Let the Story Do the Work* deftly marries the art of storytelling and the science of persuasion. With compelling insights, Choy demonstrates how to use emotion to gain the attention of any audience, even in a world crowded with so many competing messages, products, and services. I thoroughly enjoyed reading the fabric of stories Choy weaves together to illustrate the most important elements of storytelling. Her book will inspire anyone looking to break through the clutter and become the author of their own success."

—Kate Smith, Assistant Dean, Admissions and Financial Aid,
Kellogg School of Management

"I was very skeptical that Esther's storytelling techniques could make a difference for me and have an impact on engaging and enrolling an audience into my mission. After all, I had made successful business presentations for decades. BUT, the teachings in her book have made a real difference to my stakeholders and, subsequently, to me. Setting the 'hook' was a game changer. After telling one story, the audience was impressed; however, after setting the hook for a later presentation, the expressions on the faces in the audience were priceless—and the positive feedback was overwhelming. I was 'hooked' and no longer skeptical. *Let the Story Do the Work* is a powerful yet enjoyable read, and it will help your stories sing and your audience applaud!"

—Tony M. Orlando, Director, United States Auto Club

"Practical and empathetic, *Let the Story Do the Work* is an important guide for anyone seeking to improve their storytelling skills. The insightful stories Esther tells effectively teach the reader and keep the pages turning. The clear tools and step-by-step templates that she shares convert theory into action and will keep readers returning to this book time and time again."

—Stephen Shih, Former Head of MBA Career Services,
Hong Kong University of Science and Technology

"Storytelling is more important in business today than ever. It is indeed a critical skill—especially for talented entrepreneurs building the next generation of high-growth startups who share their vision with customers, investors, and potential employees every day and need to nail it. In her inspiring new book *Let the Story Do the Work*, Esther K. Choy shares countless examples from the front lines that will forever change your perception on why telling your story more effectively can be the difference between success and failure. In this book Choy provides a simple framework for bringing stories to life, along with practical recommendations on how we all can become better storytellers and be more successful in business and in our personal lives."

—Kevin Willer, Partner, Chicago Ventures

"Having recently reviewed dozens of resumes to select a handful of applicants, I now understand exactly why Esther Choy's *Let the Story Do the Work* is a must-read for anyone who wants to present him/herself to a stranger. It's impossible to fathom why one should meet a candidate based solely on a list of data on a page. More broadly, really thinking about the audience and what is likely to create a lasting impression is an invaluable exercise when presenting facts. The book is a must-read for anyone who wants to make information memorable—and who doesn't fit that description?"

—Maura O'Hara, Executive Director,
Illinois Venture Capital Association

"If your goal is to inspire others to take action, *Let the Story Do the Work* is a must-read. In a world where making sense of complex data is more crucial than ever, your audiences will greatly appreciate your newly-honed skill of connecting the dots through the magic of story. This book is filled with very practical guidance underpinned by concrete examples. Fun to read, Choy has organized each chapter and topic through stories. You'll want to turn to the next page, and the next page, and the next. . . ."

—Britta Rendlen, Head of Sustainable Finance,
World Wildlife Fund, Switzerland

"Esther Choy has figured out the primary role of story: how what we tell each other about one another, and the world around us, is the communication that binds us, and what makes the tangle of individual networks into the fabric of a society. Enjoy this useful and entertaining deconstruction, to your benefit."

—Leigh Bienen, author, Florence Kelley and the Children

"Esther Choy hits the nail on the head: 'At the heart of leadership lies persuasion. At the heart of persuasion lies storytelling.' As our world becomes more polarized, storytelling provides the ability for diverse perspectives to be understood, if not united. In this book, Choy outlines how you can improve your ability to connect with an individual or group through storytelling."

—Brian Halloran, Colonel, US Army

"Starting off in financial services, you are rewarded for your technical expertise. As you advance, you are more likely to find yourself presenting financial results to clients, pitching new project work to prospects, and coaching team members. Critical to your long-term success is your ability to tell a story. That ability enables you to connect, to persuade, and to grow your business. That's why you need Esther Choy's book. *Let the Story Do the Work* not only articulates the why of storytelling, but also provides the how—to successfully add storytelling to your professional (and personal) toolbox."

—Rissa Reddan, Chief Marketing Officer,
Performance Trust Capital Partners, LLC

"As subject matter experts, we often assume people around us are also fellow experts, and mistakenly give them an expert-level volume of details at an expert level of complexity. This spraying-and-praying approach ironically obfuscates the true value of our work in the eyes of key stakeholders. Not only does *Let the Story Do the Work* heighten our awareness to avoid this communication trap, it also provides repeatable frameworks and flexible templates so that we, the experts, can inspire and influence decision makers regardless of their level of expertise."

—Janet Kong, Head of Supply Chain Management,
Integrated Circuit Materials, Merck Group

"Just another how-to book, you think? No. An engaging, easy-to-read book from master story facilitator, Esther Choy, that will quickly draw you in with wide-ranging and absorbing stories, while simultaneously teaching and modeling Choy's valuable techniques to help you bring your own stories to life."

—Linda Akutagawa, President & CEO,
Leadership Education for Asian Pacifics, Inc.

"Success depends on engaging people's attention and having influence. Storytelling humanizes business communications—and *Let the Story Do the Work* demonstrates how to engage and influence people through storytelling. A fun read with useful tips that make you want to write down your own stories in mid-chapter."

—Julia Tang Peters, international leadership consultant, and author of
Pivot Points: Five Decisions Every Successful Leader Must Make

"Take a minute and recall the last time you were inspired and compelled to action by someone. Chances are, it was because the person gripped you with a magnificent story. In this book, Esther Choy dissects the 'art' of storytelling and transforms it into a repeatable 'science.' She then guides us through constructing our own extraordinary stories . . . that we can use to more effectively inspire and compel others to action."

—David Wong, Senior Director, Innovation & Acceleration Lab,
Chicago Mercantile Exchange Group

LET THE

story

DO THE
WORK

The Art of Storytelling for Business Success

ESTHER K. CHOY

AMACOM
AMERICAN MANAGEMENT ASSOCIATION

NEW YORK · ATLANTA · BRUSSELS · CHICAGO · MEXICO CITY · SAN FRANCISCO
SHANGHAI · TOKYO · TORONTO · WASHINGTON, DC

Bulk discounts available. For details visit:
www.amacombooks.org/go/specialsales
Or contact special sales:
Phone: 800-250-5308
E-mail: specialsls@amanet.org
View all the AMACOM titles at: www.amacombooks.org
American Management Association: www.amanet.org

Library of Congress Cataloging-in-Publication Data

Names: Choy, Esther K., author.
Title: Let the story do the work : the art of storytelling for business
  success / by Esther K. Choy.
Description: New York, NY : Amacom, [2017] | Includes bibliographical
  references.
Identifiers: LCCN 2017002502 (print) | LCCN 2017018215 (ebook) | ISBN
  9780814438022 (E-book) | ISBN 9780814438015 (hardcover)
Subjects: LCSH: Business communication. | Storytelling. | Success in business.
Classification: LCC HD30.3 (ebook) | LCC HD30.3 .C47 2017 (print) | DDC
  658.4/5--dc23
LC record available at https://lccn.loc.gov/2017002502

About AMA

American Management Association (www.amanet.org) is a world leader in talent development, advancing the skills of individuals to drive business success. Our mission is to support the goals of individuals and organizations through a complete range of products and services, including classroom and virtual seminars, webcasts, webinars, podcasts, conferences, corporate and government solutions, business books, and research. AMA's approach to improving performance combines experiential learning—learning through doing—with opportunities for ongoing professional growth at every step of one's career journey.

19 20 21 22 23 PC/LSCH 10 9 8 7 6

For Dad
The best storyteller I know.

ACKNOWLEDGMENTS

It really took a village to help me complete this book. So my deepest gratitude goes to:

All my clients, colleagues, and friends who so generously shared their work examples and personal stories so I could bring my storytelling concepts to life.

Don Norman, my mentor and design thinking professor, who put the idea of writing a book in my head—and heart—in the first place.

Brooke Vuckovic, executive coach extraordinaire, who has nudged me to step into my own spotlight.

My agent Janet Rosen at Sheree Bykofsky Associates, who believes in me and in the book's potential to enrich and enhance readers' careers.

My editor Ellen Kadin and her team at AMACOM Books, whose patient and firm guiding hands have "raised" the book to be clear, concise, and, if I may say so, brilliant.

My team Sachin Waikar, Becky Talbot, Reena Kansal, and Sara Dennison for your coaching, editing, researching, proofreading, and nerve calming.

My dear husband Bernhard Krieg for your unyielding support. Thank you for taking the kids for a whole month so I could focus on writing! What would I do without you?

Last but not least, my readers, whose affinity and curiosity for business storytelling fuel my passion for this topic. I hope this book will help you travel far and well on your career journey.

CONTENTS

INTRODUCTION: Why Stories?
How Story + Qualifications = Standout Success   xv

PART ONE:
ANATOMY OF A STORY

CHAPTER 1: Master the Principle Elements of Storytelling   3

CHAPTER 2: The Five Basic Plots in Business Communication   23

PART TWO:
BRINGING STORIES TO LIFE

CHAPTER 3: Look Who's Listening   47

CHAPTER 4: Telling Stories with Data   65

CHAPTER 5: Making the Complex Clear   89

CHAPTER 6: Combining the Power of Story and Simple Visuals   99

CHAPTER 7: Collecting Stories from Everywhere   129

PART THREE:
STORIES IN ACTION

CHAPTER 8: Using Your Own Story to Build Credibility and Connection   151

CHAPTER 9: Successful Networking Starts with a Good Story Hook   171

CHAPTER 10: Selling the Social Impact of Nonprofit
   Organizations with Story   187

CHAPTER 11: Case Study: The Healthcare Industry   203

EPILOGUE   213

Notes   215

Index   223

FOREWORD

As the Director of Alumni Career & Professional Development at the Kellogg School of Management at Northwestern University, I help our alumni find new jobs, earn promotions within their current companies, and start new businesses through coaching and workshops. Storytelling plays an integral role in all of these activities. Yet, most people struggle with telling their stories. Esther Choy's *Let the Story Do the Work* will help them tell their stories and connect with their audiences in a compelling way.

Esther's interest in storytelling began when she was an Admissions Officer for the full-time MBA program at the University of Chicago Booth School of Business. In addition to conducting admissions interviews, Esther had to train alumni and students in the process of interviewing. Most of the prospective students did not have a concise and compelling answer to the commonly asked question "Tell me about yourself." Interviewees sometimes rambled on for 15-20 minutes with unfocused monologues. (What they didn't realize is that the real question being asked was, "Tell me something about yourself that reminds me of ME?") Esther realized that people needed help with storytelling. After completing her MBA at the Kellogg School of Management at Northwestern University, Esther started her own company, Leadership Story Lab, which teaches storytelling to many clients, including quant and analytically minded business executives.

I have known Esther Choy for seven years. During that time, she has facilitated many workshops, webinars and storylabs for our alumni. She has helped clients use storytelling to connect with people to land new jobs, get promoted within their companies, gain new customers, and raise funds for their companies. I have seen Esther help corporate clients get their stories in front of investors, the media, and employees. I am honored to write this foreword for Esther's book and am gratified that a wider audience will be able to benefit from her expertise.

In *Let the Story Do the Work*, Esther starts by breaking down storytelling into its key elements to make it accessible. She uses the three-act formula to set the scene and hook the listener, then focus on the journey, and show the final resolution. Esther brings stories to life by showing you how to leverage numbers and visuals in your stories, which is so important in business. Moreover, she'll help you understand how to make complex subjects simple. And she explains how to leverage storytelling to network and build your credibility. *Let the Story Do the Work* will help you develop the storytelling skills that will enable you to achieve your professional goals.

Matthew Temple
Director, Alumni Career Services
Kellogg School of Management
Northwestern University

INTRODUCTION
Why Stories?
How Story + Qualifications = Standout Success

*I*N 2005, THE UNIVERSITY of Chicago Graduate School of Business (now known as the Booth School of Business) decided to do something unusual: offer feedback to the thousands of MBA applicants who had been denied admission. As one of six admissions officers in the full-time MBA program, I was on the hook to deliver the feedback, via fifteen-minute phone calls, to denied candidates.

I understood that top-tier business schools didn't usually share "deny feedback," and that departing from that trend was a way of offsetting the University of Chicago's reputation for being more aloof than many of our peer programs. Still, I dreaded making the calls. I didn't realize how much I would learn from the experience—or how it would set me on an entirely new professional course.

As I prepared to make my first feedback call, a scene from *Seinfeld* came to mind: George, upon hearing that yet another girlfriend was breaking up with him, exclaimed "You're giving me the it's-not-you-it's-me routine?!" That's what I expected from the candidates I called. In reality, most were receptive and gracious, and many expressed interest in using the feedback to apply the following year. I dreaded the calls less with each one completed—except for those with a specific type of candidate.

The calls I was most reluctant to make were with applicants who fit this profile: They had a GMAT score of at least 730 (out of 800; or about the 97th percentile or better), a 3.5 GPA or better in some kind of engineering from a prestigious university, strong career experience at a well-known technology firm, and recommendations that sounded genuinely praiseful. The applicants also seemed to say the right things, overall, in their essays and interviews. "Why did we deny this person?" I asked myself, slightly panicked, before those calls.

Understanding our earlier rejection decisions meant understanding the broader context in which we had made them. Specifically, while we only had to read eight or ten applications per week during the slower summer months when we made the feedback calls, during peak admissions we were reading a hundred or even more applications weekly. Like all top schools, the University of Chicago's MBA program had far more well-qualified applicants than available seats. So all the qualifications I mentioned in the previous paragraph—730 GMAT, high GPA, good work experience—didn't stand out significantly in the broader pool.

But I empathized with the applicants, many of whom seemed to believe that if they merely reiterated their resumes, regurgitating basic facts about their lives and achievements, they would cross our bar. After all, don't facts speak for themselves?

They don't, I realized, as I reviewed all those files. They don't at all.

In a competitive environment, almost everyone has strong qualifications. Almost everyone has facts in their favor. But how valuable are facts alone? Think back to the most recent lecture or presentation you attended. How many facts do you remember from it? If you're like most people, you can't recall many, if any. Chances are good, however, that you remember stories, anecdotes, and examples from the event, even if you can't think of their exact context. The average person today is inundated with facts and data, and we let most of this pass through our brains with minimal retention or reaction—unless something makes the information stand out in a meaningful way. That's where story comes in.[1]

But back in my office at the University of Chicago in the summer of 2005, I didn't yet understand that fully. What I did understand, however, was that I could appease even the most frustrated denied applicants, including those from that dreaded subset, with one simple word: "fit." As in "You are highly qualified, but you just didn't demonstrate your fit with the program as well as other applicants did."

Surprisingly, not a single one bothered to ask what exactly I meant by "fit." Maybe it was because we only had fifteen minutes. But I decided to ask the question of myself: What does "fit" mean? How do you demonstrate it? And how do you ensure that you are demonstrating your fit in ways that resonate with decision-makers?

It took me a few more years of active searching to answer these questions to my own satisfaction. But in the process, I discovered three important insights that apply far beyond the domain of business-school admissions. These insights will help you demonstrate the value you, your products, services, organizations, or causes bring, or even help you launch a new career. Most importantly, these insights will help you articulate your authenticity and value to others with unprecedented effectiveness.

THREE POWERFUL INSIGHTS

Taken together, the three insights in this section will help you understand the power of story and begin to see how to use it to your advantage in multiple arenas.

INSIGHT 1:
A Story Is Worth More than Strong Qualifications Alone

Eventually, I left my admissions position to get my own MBA (across town from the University of Chicago, but that's another story!). Going through the process and meeting my diverse classmates helped me understand something that seemed obvious in retrospect: the applicants who stand out from the crowd of fellow smart, accomplished professionals are the ones who tell the most compelling stories. More specifically, a story that connects an applicant's values, accomplishments, and future plans with the institution they are targeting will set that candidate apart in the right way. The admitted students at the University of Chicago stood out because they revealed elements of their authentic selves in a meaningful way.

I still remember the stories of several applicants we admitted to the University of Chicago. One student stood out by describing how his grandfather had bravely resisted the rule of Hitler in World War II Germany, taking great risks to protect those in danger. The applicant's vivid descriptions, and how he linked his grandfather's courage to his own values, ethics, and accomplishments, placed him in our "clear admit" group.

Another candidate told us how her large family ate dinner together every night, no matter how busy everyone was. The meals were meaningful to her not only because of the family time, but also because her parents routinely engaged their children in thoughtful discussion and debate. In her essays, she talked about how, during her campus visit, watching students and faculty discuss important business, social, and ethical issues made her feel as if she was back home, sitting at the dinner table with her family. The story went a very long way to establishing her fit with the school, and we were pleased to offer her admission.

With far fewer seats available in each class than the number of applicants, we admissions officers had to be sure that we offered admission only to applicants who truly demonstrated fit. Each of us may have had different words to describe "fit," but we all knew it when we saw it.

But competitive admissions is far from the only arena in which storytelling is the best way to integrate your values, qualifications, and aspirations.

INSIGHT 2:
We Are All in a Perpetual "Competitive Admissions" Game

Have you gone through a year-end evaluation where you had to contribute, at least in part, to assessing your own performance? Have you ever had to pitch your great idea to colleagues who weren't sure of the value you could bring? Have you had to ask friends and neighbors to donate to your breast cancer walk and found yourself wondering why people have to be asked to give to breast cancer awareness in the first place—aren't their mothers, sisters, aunts, and wives reason enough?

Hardly a day goes by when you aren't trying to inspire others to join you in some effort. But we live in an increasingly commoditized world, where even the things you hold most dearly—your ideas, projects, and causes—are commodities in someone else's eyes. The true luxury good is your audience's attention, and everyone is clamoring for it.

At the heart of leadership lies persuasion. At the heart of persuasion lies storytelling. Whether you know it or not, you engage in both daily. Competitive admission is only one example where you have to stand out however you can. Whether you are competing for a great job, seeking funding for a start-up or nonprofit, building a professional practice, or selling goods, ideas, and services, you must stand out in a strategic, authentic way. You can even think of these efforts as "lifelong mini-admissions applications." The parallels are striking: you have a lot of "competitors" in any such contest; your competitors may not even be people, but other companies, funding priorities, or endless perfect substitutions to what you're offering; you're also competing constantly for attention with other things that demand people's attention, mostly their phone screens!

Here are several examples of mini-admissions applications from different domains.

- In 2010, an investment firm was vying to be one of the first Western players to manage assets for a mainland Chinese sovereign wealth fund. But its performance record ranked it only in the middle of eight finalists. How should this firm have approached its 15-minute final presentation in Beijing?
- In 2012, a numbers-driven executive was preparing her speech to accept a lifetime contribution award from a charity at its annual gala in Chicago. She was used to giving only dry financial presentations, not heartfelt speeches aimed at

moving and inspiring audiences. How should she have
prepared?

- In 2014, the owner of a fund-management firm and major
  sponsor of an important industry conference was told that he
  would have only five minutes to discuss his company's approach
  at the conference's main luncheon in Palo Alto, California. In
  the past, he'd always had at least an hour for such presentations.
  How should he have made use of those precious minutes?

All of these are examples of people going through mini-admissions
applications, facing off against numerous competitors for the hard-
to-get attention of important decision-makers.

You may have guessed that these were all situations in which I had
the opportunity to consult and coach. In each, I showed the executives how to use the power of story to stand out and succeed: the investment firm won the mandate; the executive awardee received a
standing ovation at her gala speech; the fund administrator had a long
line of potential clients waiting to talk to him after his presentation.

How can you harness the power of storytelling in your own
mini-admissions applications?

INSIGHT 3:
You Don't Need to Be a Super Hero to Tell Great Stories

Though not a screenwriter myself, I've benefited from the wisdom of
story and screenwriting guru Robert McKee, whose former students
have included more than sixty Academy Award winners. "Given the
choice between trivial material brilliantly told versus profound material badly told," McKee wrote in his acclaimed book, *Story*, "an audience will always choose the trivial told brilliantly."[2]

This insight resonated with me immediately, and since I read it
several years ago I've shared it with as many clients as possible. Most
people, including me, aren't born master storytellers or destined to
be world-renowned super heroes and never will be. But that doesn't
mean we can't tell great stories. To convince yourself further, think
about the mountains of social science research showing that making

even subtle changes in the way we communicate can create disproportionate impact when we attempt to persuade. For example, psychologist Robert Cialdini's 35-year-long research on social influence
demonstrates that "liking" is one of the six major levers of persuasion: We tend to like those whom we perceive as being like us, and we
are more likely to say yes to them.[3] How do we make people perceive
us as being like them? By telling stories that accentuate our similari-
ties in a strategic, authentic way.

In the following chapters, I will help you learn how to stand out in
the same way I've helped countless others differentiate themselves:
by combining the art of storytelling and the science of persuasion.
With the right frameworks, tools, and practice, you can be the author
of your future success.

Here's an overview of each chapter:

PART ONE:
ANATOMY OF A STORY

1. Master the Principle Elements of Storytelling

Whether making a financial presentation or telling a personal story
in front of a crowd, the anatomies of the communication are the same.
How do you know if you are saying enough or telling so much that
you're boring people to tears? Master these fundamental elements
and you are off to a great start. The length and form of stories vary a
great deal. However, the structure, elements, characters, and anat-
omy don't.

2. The Five Basic Plots in Business Communication

There are millions of stories, as varied as storytellers' individual experiences. The most universal plots in business, however, boil down
to five. You may be practicing law or medicine, starting up a technology firm or social entrepreneurial movement, pioneering a sales
channel or the next big fundraising campaign. Learn these five basic

plots in business communication; you can save time and tap into the universal human experience.

PART TWO:
BRINGING STORIES TO LIFE

3. Look Who's Listening

This chapter shows you how to become persuasive when you tell your story through the audience's point of view—exercising an "out-of-body" technique—that showcases the storyteller's own intelligence and empathy.

4. Telling Stories with Data

Everyone is talking about Big Data and good story—separately. This chapter combines these two widely popular and essential ideas and shows you how to become an expert in both areas—seamlessly, multiplying the impact exponentially.

5. Making the Complex Clear

One of the biggest challenges of storytelling is turning very complex material into engaging narratives. Examples from the finance industry illustrate the techniques in this chapter that can simplify the most bewildering complexity.

6. Combing the Power of Story and Simple Visuals

Can you draw a line and a dot? If you say "yes," then you can tell your story much more effectively with a few simple visual elements. A picture is worth a thousand words, they say, and this chapter proves it. It will also show you multiple examples and the process of integrating storytelling and buttressing the message of the stories with simple visuals.

7. Collecting Stories from Everywhere

A Jesuit priest once said "The most sacred gift we have is our story. The second most sacred gift we have is creating a safe space for others to tell their stories." This chapter shows you how to be aggressive listeners and ask questions that will encourage your audience to share their stories. Meanings emerge and deep connections are built when we are intentional about creating intersecting stories.

PART THREE:
STORIES IN ACTION

8. Using Your Own Story to Build Credibility and Connection

When placed on the spot to say something nice about ourselves, we tend to default to vague life histories or regurgitation of our resumes. Audiences hate this! Not only is this approach redundant and offers no value (anyone can pull your information online), but it's sleep-inducing and uninspiring. This chapter teaches you how to combine the science of social influence and the art of storytelling to set an inspiring, engaging tone for every conversation and presentation.

9. Successful Networking Starts with a Good Story Hook

Many people don't get very excited by the prospect of attending a networking event. The very word "networking" conjures up images of forced smiles, instantly forgotten names, and awkward delivery of the dreaded elevator pitch. Using storytelling elements, this chapter encourages you to ditch the one-way monologue (the elevator pitch) for a high-impact pre-crafted dialogue called the elevator conversation.

10. Selling the Social Impact of Nonprofit Organizations with Story

In 2015, Americans gave $373 billion to charities. The upward trending charitable giving continues even through recession years. The largest portion came from individuals. Yet nonprofit leaders, their board members, and committed volunteers still struggle to make a case for their causes. Imagine how much more donors will give if (and when) they can make a strong case! This chapter will show you how to turn the often unwieldy and random facts and anecdotes into coherent and donor-centric stories.

11. Case Study: The Healthcare Industry

Healthcare is a highly specialized industry, in which explanations are often filled with incomprehensible jargon. Meet five healthcare executives who, through the use of story, are able to motivate and inspire their employees and reassure patients through clear and empathetic explanations.

I've written this book specifically with you in mind. You, the people in the ranks of leadership in corporate, academic, and nonprofit organizations, have been promoted (perhaps again!) to lead. You might actually be oh-so-close to joining the C-suite or top management team. You have gotten to where you are through ambition, analytical prowess, and hard work. You have been schooled in the "just the facts, ma'm" approach and are more comfortable working with Microsoft Excel's ribbon than tying a ribbon to a birthday gift.

But wait! You may very well be at the cusp of what the well-known Peter Principle describes as "reaching the point of your incompetence." The ground has shifted. Your junior team members are now handling the quantitative and analytical work. You now are in charge of communicating, guiding, coaching, explaining, defending, influencing, and persuading. Your career now hinges upon your ability to tell stories—about yourself, your team, and your organization—in the most compelling way to a wide range of audiences: teammates, superiors, other colleagues, customers, prospects, partners, investors, regulators, and the general public. Note that using story more effectively will also deepen your relationship with people outside of work, from family to friends.

As I mentioned earlier, you don't need to be a super hero to tell great stories. All you need are tools, frameworks, examples, and practice. In the following chapters, you will find everything you need to shine when you find yourself in the spotlight. I believe that the classical approach to storytelling can elevate everyday business communication from autopilot exchanges to authentic, persuasive, and action-prone conversations. I invite you to discover the transformational power of this time-honored approach with me!

YOU'RE ON!

ANATOMY OF A STORY

CHAPTER 1

MASTER THE KEY ELEMENTS OF STORYTELLING

*I*N SPRING 2016, A small art museum in Cincinnati, Ohio, was preparing for a critical meeting. The museum was about to launch a capital campaign and needed several major donors to pledge six-figure gifts to give momentum to the fundraising effort. After months of extensive research and networking, the campaign director secured an initial meeting with a well-known banker. This potential donor was of course a very busy person, and promised only fifteen minutes to the director while he was in town for business. Knowing the initial conversation could make or break the chance of a sizable gift, the campaign director asked the museum's lead curator to join the meeting to discuss the museum's impact on Cincinnati and its community.

Thrilled and nervous, the lead curator wanted to be as prepared for the meeting as possible. So she drafted what she wanted to say, asked colleagues for feedback, invited the content manager to edit her "speech," then rehearsed it over and over. On the morning of the meeting, however, the banker's executive assistant called to inform the museum that there had been a schedule change and he had only five minutes to meet with them!

Now, if you were this museum curator, what would you do? How would you change your plan to use that five minutes most effectively?

Our museum curator cared deeply for her work and believed wholeheartedly in the organization's mission. She had spent days preparing her speech, chosen each word carefully, and rehearsed to the point that she could practically recite it in her sleep. So, rather than cutting it down or synthesizing it, she rushed through it, delivering a fifteen-minute talk in the allotted five minutes.

Put yourself in the banker's shoes and imagine what he might have heard. That's right: absolutely nothing! The curator spoke so quickly that nothing stuck, other than the idea that her approach was not effective. The banker left the meeting without any motivation to make a large pledge. He probably even wondered why he had agreed to the meeting to begin with. At the time of this writing, the museum was still trying to schedule a follow-up conversation with the banker. But its leaders recognized that they had squandered a critical early opportunity.[1]

In a world where time is scarce, attention spans minuscule, and information abundant, how do we find a way to inform and influence others most effectively? How can you use a compelling, memorable story to sway and persuade others important to your mission or goals?

Doing this right requires seeing business communication in a broader context to understand where, how, and why storytelling fits in.

"STORY" IS EVERYWHERE NOW, BUT WHAT EXACTLY IS IT?

One spring morning, while I was driving to work, a radio ad caught my attention. "Tell your business story," it said. Since storytelling is my business, I sat up a little straighter and listened closely. The ad continued: "For standout business cards, stickers, and flyers, go to our website. . . ." What started out sounding like a pitch for a company

Fig 1-1

or service similar to mine turned out to be an ad for an online printing company using the trendy term "story" to catch people's attention!

I shouldn't have been surprised. I run into examples like this almost daily. Take a look at this flyer I came across at a private club in downtown Chicago around Easter a year ago (see Figure 1-1).

"Bring the Story Home," suggests the headline. Based on that phrase, I imagined a small group of people huddling together, talking, reflecting, sharing their stories in a warm, welcoming home setting. But the flyer was merely advertising the centerpiece for an Easter-themed brunch. There's nothing wrong with urging guests to buy a memento from a special occasion, but the use of the word "story" here was again largely misguided.

Story is not a business card or sticker. Story is not an Easter Bunny centerpiece. Nor is it any of the things below, in and of themselves:

- Monologue
- Anecdote
- Pitch (including sales and elevator pitches)
- Presentation
- Product

- Service
- Cause
- Assumption
- Selling conversation
- Thesis (such as a research thesis or investment thesis)

While story can—and should—be incorporated into many of these items, they do not represent story on their own. It is only when you integrate the use of story into these types of communications that you can drive amazing results.

CORE COMPONENTS OF A STORY

To recognize a true story, look for the core components common to all stories with business impact:

- Structural: A story has a beginning, middle, and end.
- Elemental: A story often has elements including a hero, challenge, journey, resolution, change, and call to action.
- Authentic: A story reveals a genuine part of the teller, which elicits emotion in the audience.
- Strategic: A story sparks an audience's imagination, causes them to relate to the situation in the story, and motivates them to act.

By this definition, a story with business impact can be as short as one sentence. Or it can be a three-minute introduction or a thirty-minute product demonstration. Whatever the case, it will have maximum impact if it includes the components above strategically.

Throughout this book, we will be revisiting these core components of effective stories. In the following sections, we focus on two elements at the heart of these components: emotion and audience.

CONSIDER YOUR STORY'S EMOTIONAL QUALITY

Story and emotion share a critical link you need to use.

What makes you decide something or take action? It's tempting to say that facts, data, or observable evidence guide our decision-making and actions, with very little role played by emotion. In reality, emotion is not only necessary but plays a key role in our decision-making process, as highlighted by many recent writers across fields, including the Heath brothers in their excellent book *Switch*.[2]

Meet "Elliot," a hardworking accountant who was living the American Dream in the early 1980s.[3] Unfortunately, he developed a brain tumor in his orbitofrontal cortex, requiring surgery. The procedure seemed to have gone well, as Elliot retained what appeared to be all of his physical, linguistic, and intellectual capacities. But soon it was clear that he'd lost something post-surgery: his ability to make decisions, even about the simplest things. Merely choosing between a black or blue pen to sign a document could take him over thirty minutes. The underlying reason was that Elliot had lost the ability to connect emotion with decision-making; the surgery had cut him off from his "emotional mind," making him "pathologically indecisive."

Emotions are critical to our ability to decide in many situations. As Alan Weiss noted in his book *Million Dollar Consulting*, "Logic makes people think, emotion makes them act."[4] This can be especially true when we're faced with many similar-seeming options. "Go with your gut" is valid advice in such cases, as long as your emotion is well-informed by some set of facts or experience. That's true in business, as well.

Di Fan Liu is an onshore private banker based in Beijing. He and his firm serve ultra-rich Chinese entrepreneurs, mostly founders of publicly traded China-based companies. Widely admired, these first-generation trailblazers overcame highly restrictive economic policies in past decades to succeed, and many retain active control of their businesses. Yet most of them struggle with the issue of how best to pass their wealth on to their family's next generations. That's where Mr. Liu and his bank come into the picture.

In speaking with these high-value prospects, Liu and his colleagues rarely talk about what the bank has to offer, at first (I'll explain this strategy in the last story). Instead, they tell stories. Specifically, they relate narratives about how other multi-generation family businesses worldwide have dealt successfully with ownership succession, whether in the US, EU, Latin America, or elsewhere—such as a US-based real estate family that has passed wealth down to three generations using a set of complex but fair trusts. Then they ask their prospective clients to think of a fellow Chinese entrepreneur who'd successfully passed on wealth to the next generation. The vast majority can't think of even one. Next, Liu shares an important observation: since an economic downturn happens every seven to eight years on average, in any given century a person could lose their wealth as many as fourteen times. Finally, he asks them: "What are you doing to protect your wealth and legacy?"

You can imagine how Liu's prospects may feel after the conversation: grateful for the new knowledge, but also vulnerable and a bit frustrated, knowing that other leaders like them have succeeded where they are struggling, and the risks are quite high. The emotions make them receptive to hearing how Liu and his bank can help them, and that's exactly what Liu tells them now.

The idea is that your story, no matter how well told, can't achieve its full intended effect until you embed within it an emotional quality aligned with your purpose. Remember: logic makes you think; emotion makes you act. How can you build the right emotional quality into your story to create the desired impact?

In the next section, we will explore how to better understand the emotions of our audiences.

KNOW YOUR AUDIENCE INSIDE AND OUT

In an ideal world, you the storyteller can take your time and convey everything you want to in whatever amount of time you need—just as the museum curator in our opening example wished. In reality, what we say, how we say it, and when we say it are constrained by a big factor: our audience's needs and reactions.

When most people are preparing to tell their stories, they tend to think only about what they will tell and how they will tell it. Too often they neglect to think about how their audience will react to the stories, as influenced by their own needs and preferences. Remember: large ambition, hard work, and even impressive credentials are not sufficient to succeed in most business contexts today. A hallmark of an effective leader is whether she can convince others—her audiences—to follow her as related to vision, strategy, tactics, or any other area. That means leaders have to understand their audiences' needs and constraints, to decide how to communicate with them most effectively.

In chapter 3, we will explore in depth how to connect with an audience. The framework below, however, is a start that will help you understand your audience better by breaking down what happens to them during any presentation or interaction into two levels: internal and external. This "inside and out" approach will help you prepare much more effective presentations.

Internal

What happens to your audience internally, or inside, involves what they feel and what they know.

Feel. The famed American writer and activist Maya Angelou once said, "I've learned that people will forget what you said, people will forget what you did, but people will never forget how you made them feel." Often overlooked in business contexts, not only does emotion have a high "sticky" factor, but it also plays a critical and necessary role in decision-making. Whether we intend it or not, our audiences will experience a specific emotion—intrigued, bored, happy, unsettled, excited, apathetic, surprised, confused, or some combination—after listening to us. But note that they may not be able to articulate their feelings even if you press them to share. Still, they are definitely feeling something! This emotion can affect how long, if at all, they will remember what you've just told them, and what, if anything, they are willing to do about it. So wiser communicators always try to predict how their message would make audiences feel, and alter messages that may not result in the hoped-for emotion.

Know. Whether you are presenting at an industry conference or conversing with your manager during a mid-afternoon coffee break, you want your audience to come away from the interaction knowing something they didn't before. Maybe you're showing conference attendees (potential clients) how to generate consumer insights from massive amounts of hospitality data. Or maybe you're apprising your manager about a competitor firm's rumored product research. Transmitting that information is critical because knowledge is power, as they say. Unfortunately, we live in a data-overloaded world where most information is quickly commoditized and information without sufficient context or stickiness is quickly forgotten. So you have to be highly strategic about how you present the information you want your audience to retain. The vehicle for your message matters—a lot.

External

The external factor has to do with what questions your audience asks and whether—and how—they act as a consequence of what you've presented them.

Ask. Feeling and knowing, discussed above, take place internally, within members of your audience. But effective communication will yield an external sign of their interest: they will ask questions. "Tell me more about that data analysis approach," they might say. Or "What's the best reaction to our competitor's new product research?" Regardless of the form, a question means your audience wants to know more. Follow-up questions are the number one indicator that you have created real interest in your listeners, which makes them want more information, insights, opinions, and recommendations— all things that it's better to have them ask for than for you as the presenter to dump on them unsolicited. Questions indicate that you've created the opportunity for a real dialogue, rather than a one-way monologue. That means a central objective of your story is to inspire questions in your audience. (As you might have guessed, this would have been a better strategy for that museum curator when she found out that she had less than half the expected time to communicate with the banker and potential donor.)

Act. Unlike writing a novel or memoir, or getting on stage to communicate a personal narrative at one of the increasingly popular storytelling events in the US, telling a story is almost always aimed at influencing others to act, to effect change. When people tell personal stories and show their vulnerability in front of a crowd of strangers, they are sharing something they feel compelled to, possibly hoping to evince emotion in audience members. But the goal of a story told in a business context is to inspire action, no matter how big or small. For example, say you and several friends are creating a food-delivery app, but it's not quite ready for launch. So your goal at this stage is to recruit beta-testers. You could first share an origin story (see next chapter) and your basic business model with friends and colleagues, then ask them to act: "You're in our target market, and your personal habits can help us develop the best app possible. Could you commit to downloading it and testing it by the end of the month?" A good story will help inspire the desired action.

PRINCIPAL ELEMENTS OF STORYTELLING

Below are the five Principal Elements of Storytelling. We'll return to these repeatedly throughout the book, so I want to present a full description of each up front here.

The Three-Act Formula

When you visit a store or restaurant or movie theater, do you worry that the floor will collapse and send you crashing to the level below? At home, do you constantly question whether the roof will fall on you? Hopefully not! These questions may sound ridiculous (at least in more developed countries), but I'm using them to point out the importance of structure.

Structure is critical not only to buildings, but also to stories. When the structure of a building is solid, we don't question it. In fact, we don't even think about it, because we don't have to. When something works, we tend not to even notice it. Same goes for story structure, which holds all the elements together, usually without your realizing it. In fact, all strong stories share the same basic structure: the Three-Act Formula.

Whether it's your favorite novel, sitcom, or movie, the story presented can almost always be broken into three parts, or acts. In Act I, you are oriented to the time, place, and setting of the story. You meet the main characters, and ideally you are intrigued by what is about to happen next because there is a hook (see below) at the end of the act. Act I is typically the shortest part of the story because the hook needs to work its magic as soon as possible, lest the story lose the audience's precious interest. Then Act II represents the main journey of the story. This is usually the longest part of any story, including large and small setbacks, moments of clarity, newfound insights, and known and unknown obstacles. Toward Act II's end, the protagonist typically meets the biggest challenge head-on. In Act III, we see how she overcomes it. As the challenge is resolved, the lead character and her situation also have changed, typically for the better. This leads to a final, satisfying ending and resolution.

Since the Three-Act Structure is so important, let's walk through it again below, using the well-known movie *The Sound of Music* as an example.

In Act I, we meet the main character(s). In *The Sound of Music*, gifted songstress and nun-in-training Maria is the main character, and we first meet her singing on a gorgeous mountaintop in the Alps pre-World War II, on the eve of the Anschluss in 1938. Then we're presented with the hook that the filmmakers hope will keep us interested in the movie for its duration. As the audience soon discovers, the hook is that Maria's not at all sure that she's found the right calling, and we understand that this will be tested when she agrees to become governess for the von Trapp family. The journey begins.

In Act II, things usually get complicated, and the main character faces a series of tests/obstacles as part of their journey. In Maria's case, that means struggling to win the von Trapp childrens' acceptance and, later, the affections of the captain, who is already beholden to the Baroness Schrader. After multiple tribulations, Maria understands better who she is (hint: not a nun!), but now she and the von

Trapps face the danger of falling into Nazi hands. This act usually ends with the question of whether the hero can survive—literally or figuratively—and reach a fulfilling resolution against growing, seemingly insurmountable odds.

Act III typically answers all central questions of the story and brings the main character—and the audience—to a fulfilling resolution. In *The Sound of Music*, the von Trapps elude the Nazis and sail off into the figurative sunset, or hike into a beautiful mountain setting, in this case. Fade to black. Love wins.

The Hook.

"Plant a good hook early in your story to grab your audience's attention" is easy to say, but it may be difficult to do. So, how do you create a strong hook? While there are innumerable potentially valid hooks, a more systematic way to create one—even when you don't feel particularly creative—is to follow the "3 Cs": **conflict**, **contrast**, and **contradiction**. I'll define these, then present examples. Simply put, a *conflict* is the clash of forces or needs going in opposite directions. But note that a conflict need not be epic, such as war or famine. A conflict could simply be about an argument between spouses or a person desperately wanting to fall asleep but unable to. A *contrast* typically involves the juxtaposition of two opposite qualities: heavy and light, plentiful and meager, active and apathetic; the list goes on. A *contradiction* goes against the expectation of your audiences. The examples below are from the beginnings of stories my clients wrote. See if you can tell whether/how each represents a conflict, contrast, or contradiction.

EXAMPLE 1

"Things had started badly on June 21, 2002, with England losing to Brazil in the Football World Cup, and they had steadily been getting worse; that fateful day ended up with our being finally rescued by the Navy."

Circle what you think is the right answer:

CONFLICT   CONTRAST   CONTRADICTION

EXAMPLE 2

"I was born and raised in New York City. I consider myself a New Yorker before I call myself an American. Yet, several years ago, my job brought me to a small desert village in Sudan."

Circle what you think is the right answer:

CONFLICT   (CONTRAST)   CONTRADICTION

EXAMPLE 3

"It was Tuesday at 10:03 a.m., my second day on a new job. Chris, a software developer, was explaining the company's technology to me. In the middle of our conversation, he received an instant message. He quickly got up and told me 'It's time for a cupcake run!'"

Circle what you think is the right answer:

CONFLICT   CONTRAST   (CONTRADICTION)

Now let's discuss. Example 1 is primarily a classic *conflict*. In fact, there are two levels of conflict in this beginning to a much longer story. First, in any competitive team sport, one team opposes the other. Both teams want to win, but only one can. But the opening also implies a second conflict. When you are well and safe, the last thing that comes to mind is needing someone to rescue you, especially not the Navy! So, embedded in this story is the idea of a conflict between the need to survive and a life-threatening event or force. Thus most listeners would ask "Just want kind of trouble is the storyteller in that would require the Navy to intervene?" Many clients also suggest that this hook reflects a contradiction as well: Why would someone watching the World Cup all of a sudden find their life in peril and need the Navy? Indeed, this hook can also be a contradiction. Any hook may be one or more of the 3 C's!

Example 2 is a *contrast*. Even if you've never been to New York City or Sudan, you can easily envision the stark difference between a bustling metropolis and a barren, sparsely populated desert village. The contrast is immediate and powerful.

Example 3 is best viewed as a *contradiction*. In most work settings, one does not exit a conversation with a new colleague so abruptly just to go buy desserts!

Regardless of the exact type of hook represented, all three examples make us wonder exactly what is going on in the story, and make us want to know more. That's exactly what your hook should do: get your audience interested and eager to hear more.

Challenge and Change.

"Super confident people with no problems and great marriages and great parenting are not good entertainment," said Matthew Weiner, creator of the hit TV series *Mad Men*.[5] Weiner, like any great TV, film, or advertising leader, knows that challenges create interest, which in turn motivates sustained attention from the audience. Having a central challenge in your story also creates change, in the main characters, in their situations, or (ideally) both. If challenge is the nerve center of a story, then change is the soul of it. If everyone or everything remains the same at the story's end, then what's the point of the journey? Audiences innately want to know not just what happened in the story, but what's different at the end, and why.

A Clear Theme

When asked to introduce yourself at a panel discussion or similar event, what do you usually say? Most likely your introduction is full of facts (where you're from, education credentials, work history) following a basic chronological order. Unfortunately, recounting events or qualifications—no matter how impressive they might be—is not the same as telling a story. A story needs a theme, and chronology is not a sufficient one. In order for listeners to understand and appreciate the story theme, the storyteller must tell his stories by weaving events and reflection together. In a recent *Fortune* article, Alex Baydin, CEO of PerformLine, shared what he learned when his company almost went bankrupt.[6] He writes: "[W]orse than all of [the] rejections [from venture capitalists] was the idea that the one thing I'd vowed to never allow as founder and CEO seemed like a serious possibility: I might miss a payroll." Baydin could have just dumped this detail on us: "It looked like I was going to miss a payroll." But instead, he blends in what it meant to him to be unable to pay his employees. He has reflected on his experience, and we can tell! We can see Baydin's values as he relates this unsettling event, and that speaks to a theme of striving to live by one's values, even despite major obstacles. That's much more meaningful to the audience.

Open or Closed End?

Ten years ago, my colleague Reena Kansal's mother and uncle cajoled her into seeing a fortune teller in Mumbai. Trained as an engineer and deeply analytical by nature, Reena found the idea of some sage she'd never met having special access to her past and future beyond ludicrous. Yet she was blown away, as she tells the story today, by how much detail this fortune teller knew about her life and how many things he predicted that turned out to be true, simply because he told her "I have found your book." Reena told this story to many different audiences, and at the end she would ask each: "Do you believe that there is a book out there somewhere about your life? That your life story has already been written and will unfold as intended?"

This ending is no accident. I brainstormed this story with Reena deeply, and we agreed that an Open End, one that turns the next part of the story over to the audience, is the best way to conclude.

Whether it is open or closed, the last part of your story in any setting is crucial and needs to be the result of a conscious decision. What are you trying to achieve with your story? What do you hope your listeners will do upon hearing your stories? For Reena, she truly does not know what to make of her bizarre experience with the fortune teller years ago. So she is curious to hear what other people think. Perhaps they have had similar encounters and can help shed light on her experience. Perhaps they are fortune tellers themselves or know some fortune-telling secrets to share.

In general, we know that by intentionally leaving the end of the story open, we are inviting others to share their stories. One thing I haven't yet told you about my colleague and fellow storyteller Reena is that she is a classic introvert. She would rather listen than talk. She used to hate going to networking events, always struggling with what to say to someone new. But when she tells this fortune-telling story, she gets to *listen* more than she has to talk because she creates an inviting, open space for others to share their stories. Consequently, she builds memorable relationships at networking and other events using the communication style that suits her personally much better than a more closed-ended elevator pitch would. (We talk about the elevator pitch in Chapter 9.)

But there are situations in which your story will be more effective with a Closed End. For example, say you and your team are developing a new insurance product and thinking of strategic ways to encourage a target group of medical professionals to buy the policy, even though they're not bound to do so by law. In your favor, recent statistics show that these professionals are bearing disproportionate financial risk when they practice without the extra protection. So you set out to tell a story of someone who did not think she needed the special insurance but ended up being sued, lost, and was forced to file for bankruptcy. At the end of this story, there should be little doubt about what these medical professionals should do: buy the additional policy. As the storyteller, though, it's easy to fall into thinking that that's so obvious, you don't have to say it. Don't make that mistake. Quite often, teachers are surprised what students remember in their lectures that they, the teachers, deem inconsequential. Similarly, many of my clients are surprised that their audiences "just don't get it." More often than not, people don't get it because the takeaways were never clear. So our insurance story should end with something like: "That's why we're excited to bring this product to you, to prevent you from suffering a similar outcome."

In short, be thorough in your approach to endings. Whether you go with Open or Closed, consider the desired results you wish to see in your listeners. Is there a specific set of actions you hope they will take? Are you trying to sway opinions? Or are you intending to create an exchange, a dialogue, to collect stories? Whatever the outcome might be, craft the end of your story accordingly, and with care.

THREE RULES OF SMART STORYTELLING

When telling any kind of story for any purpose, keep the following rules in mind.

Know when to intrigue and delight or data dump?

There are times when we need just to whet our audiences' appetite, and there are times we want, or need, to share a lot of information with them. So, before you start talking, ask yourself this question: Is it more urgent and important that I intrigue and delight them, or that I inform them? If it's just one of those two, build your story around that goal. If it's both, think about how best to sequence the material, based on your audience's needs.

Know the difference between proving and persuading

Do your audiences need numbers, data, and facts—or just love communications based on these? Or are they motivated more by emotional material, with facts secondary or even unimportant? The former may be true when speaking to a highly analytical audience, such as scientists or R&D managers. The latter may be especially true during an election year or a hotly contested referendum. Think the Clinton–Trump election of 2016, or the controversial "Brexit" (the UK's 2016 vote to leave the EU). One of these audiences will respond better to proving (using facts and analytical process to generate truth), while the other will look to be persuaded by emotionally laden information. Understanding what your particular listeners need is the first step of winning them over.

Understand that the story of you isn't about you

Many times the stories we tell, personal or professional, come from our own experience. That makes it too easy to shift the focus of our stories from the audiences to ourselves. Resist that temptation. A story with business impact should ultimately be about the audience and their needs; they will know what to do with your story and will benefit most from it, rather than the other way around. Make it about them. We'll talk in detail about connecting with the audience in chapter 3.

ALWAYS FILL STORY VACUUMS

At this point, you're probably thinking that crafting an effective story in a business context sounds like a lot of work. If so, you're right! Mining, refining, and telling a compelling story can take time and effort, especially if you're not used to this way of communication—and most people aren't. So, to motivate yourself to take on this potentially daunting task, think about what happens if we don't tell stories. What if we just present numbers and other facts in a more basic form and let the audience decide what they mean and what to do about them?

In other words, what happens in a "story vacuum?" In the absence of a narrative, especially in an ambiguous and/or urgent situation, people will seek out and consume plausible stories like water in the desert. It is our innate nature to connect the dots. Moreover, once an explanatory narrative is adopted, it's extremely hard to undo. Take the dubious connection between autism and vaccination. In the US, autism has been on the climb since the 1970s.[7] It's an understandably distressing, desperate situation for those affected and their families. Naturally, they ask questions. Why are there so many more cases of autism now? What caused this? Then, in 1998, a scientist named Andrew Wakefield published a study that established a link between autism and vaccines in *The Lancet*, a well-respected British medical journal.[8] Now imagine that your child or that of someone close to you is autistic. How would you react to this finding? For many, the discovery became gospel and they became staunchly opposed to vaccinations, the companies that make them, and the government bodies that defend their merits. But a few years later, Wakefield admitted that he had fabricated the whole study! In theory, this revelation should have motivated the anti-vaccination crowd to do a 180-degree turn. But it didn't. In the intervening years, even though dozens of studies were conducted on this very same question and established zero link between autism and vaccines, it failed to change many minds among the opposition. They were sticking to the story they initially believed. (Wakefield himself has since been disbarred in the UK.)

Once a story has taken root in hearts and minds, it's extremely difficult to challenge its validity. As a leader, if you don't connect the dots proactively, if you don't fill the vacuum with your story, others will fill it in for you. And you may lose your opportunity to influence your audiences. So do your best to fill any important story vacuum, ideally with a fact-based story, as we discuss below.

ESTABLISH FACT-BASED STORIES

In summer 2014, oil prices began a precipitous drop from slightly above $100 per barrel to about $50 per barrel by 2016.[9] The decline, especially in the beginning, was puzzling. The fundamental law of supply and demand—such as a drop in demand or an increase in supply sources—didn't fully explain it. As a result, few could offer any reliable prediction about when and where oil prices would stabilize. There was a yawning story vacuum. So Florence Fitzerald (not her real name), senior partner of a global investment firm, took a step back and thought about other plausible explanations. She sought to fill the story vacuum for investors and other key audiences.

First, Fitzerald did extensive research. She looked at the deterioration of Syria and the accompanying fallout between the US and Russia. She read reports on the potential nuclear deal between the US and Iran, a deal that naturally upset Saudi Arabia. And since the Saudis had known for quite some time that the US could eventually produce enough shale gas to become more energy-independent, she connected the dots into a plausible story: the Saudis had intentionally flooded the market with oil supply to establish a stronger market share before the US could increase its share with its own greater supply. The Saudis' move represented a proxy economic war with Iran and Russia and a signal to the US that they would not view a nuclear deal with Iran and the inevitable lift of economic sanctions favorably.

She tested her story by monitoring how often the Saudi government, on Al-Jazeera News, had been telling its people to get used to oil prices being lower and for longer periods. When you have this kind of proxy economic war, Fitzerald reasoned, you cannot predict oil prices, but you may be able to make other valuable inferences about political and economic events/outcomes.

Although not all her clients bought this story, that's not the point. More important is that at a time of great uncertainty, Fitzerald's story gave her audiences an alternative, plausible viewpoint. Her story gave them another possible way to connect the dots and make sense of an ambiguous situation with implications for them. Her explanation gave them a new way to think about and analyze a problem that they did not know how to solve or react to, strengthening their trust in her and deepening the relationship.

THE THREE STAGES OF COMMUNICATION MASTERY

How do you become a master communicator? Is it the use of flowery language and commanding gestures? Not really. Is it about a strong presence and being articulate? These qualities certainly help, but they are not enough. Master communicators tend to have successfully completed three stages of development that most of us haven't. Here they are:

Stage 1: Before we accumulate significant work experience, our resumes look sparse and our leadership roles, if any, tend to come through extracurricular activities. Naturally, we are more likely to take a back seat to our superiors at work and let them do most or all of the talking. This is the first stage, where everyone begins.

Stage 2: Over time, we move up the career ladder. We gain more knowledge and use that to develop insights and establish points of view about our industries, as related to trends, outlook, strategy, and tactics. We share our knowledge and ideas more frequently, both formally (presentations, speeches, panels) and informally (mentorship conversations). The more we know, the more frequently we tend to speak. But many of us never progress beyond this second stage.

Stage 3: This most challenging stage to reach involves making sense of highly complex issues in a world where information and implications grow with unprecedented speed and volume, and expertise must necessarily be more nuanced. There never seems to be enough time to convey what we know. In stage three, a few true master communicators emerge. They can simplify without dumbing down. They can distill complex ideas to their core essence. They can get novice audiences to understand, follow, and appreciate complicated topics. They can get audiences of all levels of sophistication to ask for more and to take action. They do so through telling stories. You can become a master communicator by honing your storytelling skills!

This all sounds really good, you may think. But you're a busy person with only limited time to learn storytelling, which probably seems very time-consuming, based on this chapter! Many of my clients have raised that exact concern. "It does take time," I tell them. I also assure them that there are ways to be more efficient—to jump-start the process. For example, there are five basic business plots that anyone can understand and relate to. In the next chapter, I will describe what these five plots are and provide you with outlines that will get you crafting your stories immediately.

CHAPTER 2

THE FIVE BASIC PLOTS IN BUSINESS COMMUNICATION

HAS THIS EVER HAPPENED to you? You turn on Netflix and *Making of a Murderer* is on. Just as you start the latest episode, you realize you're thirsty. No problem, you tell yourself, you can grab a glass of water when there's a break in the story. But before you even realize it, the episode's over, and for the first time in an hour you remember your thirst. Or maybe this sounds familiar: You finally decide to read the book *Eat, Pray, Love* because your friends have been urging you to for years. You open the book in the early evening and before you know it, it's midnight and you have a 4 a.m. conference call with a client in London the next day. How did this happen?

We've all experienced something like the examples above. That's because when we hear a good story, we lose track of time. Hours can go by without our noticing, as if time has gotten compressed. Why is that? Sure, an effective hook will intrigue you; we have to be interested in the basic premise of a story to attend to it. But even that doesn't guarantee that what happens next will keep our attention, preventing us from looking at our watches or turning to the last few pages.

What keeps us interested in stories often boils down to one word: plot. Plot is the sequence of events—and ideally twists, turns, and mysteries—in your story. A story that holds us spellbound and compresses time almost always has a significant number of turning events. This isn't just speculation, but science. Behavioral scientist Paul Dolan, for example, observed that "It appears as if our brains actually calculate time based on the number of events that occur; so the more events, the more time we feel has passed."[1]

As you can imagine, there are thousands of potential plots, especially if you include subtle details, such as the exact murder weapon used in the exact location by the specific perpetrator (remember the board game *Clue*?). But when it comes to business stories, I have found that there are really only Five Basic Plots.[2] Why should you care? Why confine yourself to these five plots? Two reasons. One, these five plots recur repeatedly because they speak to a certain universality of experience and understanding among us humans. Two, life is full of random events. It is up to us, as the storytellers, to organize these chaotic experiences into themes and a logical (but not predictable) order—the spine of story—which makes it easier for readers to follow, retain, and be influenced by the story, much more so than if it were a random chain of events. These five plots give us blueprints for what our narrative theme and sequence of events might look like. Of course, you do not have to limit yourself to these five plots forever. Knowing what they are, however, can jump-start your story crafting and give you a solid foundation from which to be more creative. Know the rules before you break them, right?

WHAT PLOTS LOOK LIKE

Before we dive into the details of the five plots, let's consider plot visually (or a "plot of a plot"), to enhance our understanding. To do this, we turn to well-known author Kurt Vonnegut (*Slaughterhouse-Five*, *Cat's Cradle*, and many others) and his brilliant graphical interpretation of story. In his essay collection *A Man Without a Country*, Vonnegut gives a master lesson on creative writing, using the x- and y-axes as his teaching tool.[3] Here, the x-axis represents the passage of time; the y-axis represents fortune, as shown in the figure below.

Man in a Hole

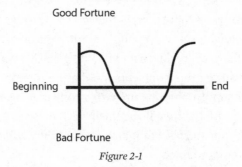

Figure 2-1

Many stories start their main character out with good fortune but then plunge them into trouble or misfortune, from which they typically recover. Vonnegut called these Man-in-a-Hole stories (of course they can be Woman- or Child- or Animal-in-a-Hole stories too!), with plots as represented in this simple figure. (See Figure 2-1.)

Vonnegut also describes the Boy-Meets-Girl story or plot. Note that it does not need to be about an actual boy meeting an actual girl. Rather, at its most basic level it is a story about an average person on a more or less average day who unexpectedly finds something (or someone) wonderful, but then loses it. Will his hard work to win it back succeed? In most conventional stories, it will, as pretty much every romantic comedy film in history tells us! But the visual for this plot looks different from the Man-in-a-Hole graph, as in this figure (see Figure 2-2).

Boy Meets Girl

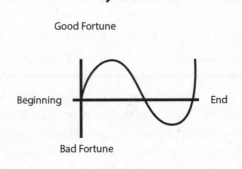

Figure 2-2

Vonnegut continues with two more distinct plots: the Cinderella story, and Shakespeare's *Hamlet*.[4] We won't cover those in detail here, but the basic idea is that though characters, settings, and conflicts might differ considerably, strikingly similar patterns may be found across the millions of stories that exist in the world at any given point. So, whether you're preparing a business pitch, speaking at a conference panel, or simply catching up with a colleague over lunch, familiarize yourself with the Five Basic Business Plots. Not only will it help you construct your stories, but it ensures that they will resonate more deeply with your audience.

THE FIVE BASIC PLOTS

Here we'll cover the five basic business story plots in detail, so you can think about how to apply them to the pursuit of your goals.

Origin

Humans have a shared desire to know how things began—whether the universe, a specific event, or even ourselves. "Mommy, where did I come from?" is a perfectly natural—if horror-inducing for parents—question that most children ask in some form. An origin story—which all of these are—can instill a sense of identity and heritage, place an event or person in historical context, or simply satisfy deep curiosity. So it's no surprise that every religion and culture has its own origin story about how the world formed and how its people came to be.

In business, an origin story might be a founder's story, or how a person, business, idea, product, service, platform, movement, or opportunity came to be. Let's look at an example. In 2006, people had lots of questions for Indra Nooyi. Why? Because this native of India had just become the first female CEO of PepsiCo and the first non–US-born CEO of a major US company. Becoming the first of anything—whether the first of your family to attend college, the first person to swim the Atlantic, or the first person to discover that ulcers are caused by bacteria, not stress—often leads to the question of *how*. How did this happen? In Nooyi's case, the most frequent question was "How did you get here?" She addressed the question with an origin story that she retold at the 92Y conference in New York.[5]

Nooyi said about her elementary-school years, "Every night at the dinner table, my mother would ask us to write a speech about what we would do if we were president, chief minister, or prime minister— every day would be a different world leader she'd ask us to play.... At the end of dinner, we had to give the speech, and she had to decide who she was going to vote for." Although this ritual might make her household sound like a scary place in which to grow up, Nooyi, her sister, and her mother all had fun with this evening routine, and they used it as a way to learn and grow. Importantly, the speeches prepared the sisters to present and defend arguments, including against tough questions. Later in her career, when Nooyi found her male colleagues consistently double-checking her answers with other male colleagues, she would call them out on their action and make clear the validity of her original ideals and recommendations, handling their questions and skepticism effectively. In the context of this origin story, Nooyi's rise makes even more sense, as she was raised from an early age to think for herself, back up her arguments, and even to believe she could be the head of any state (or company)!

Rags to Riches

This is probably one of the most common business stories. Think about how many stories there are of self-made millionaires who came from humble backgrounds. Horatio Alger became a highly successful author in the 19th century, peddling exactly these kinds of stories in his books. A variant of rags to riches is the David-versus-Goliath story, or what many know as the underdog story. Whatever you call it, this plot is about someone who starts from a very low station in life, without much hope for improvement, but surprises everyone with a dramatic turnaround. If Vonnegut were to graph such a plot, it would look something like Figure 2-3.

Rags to Riches

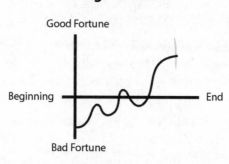

Figure 2-3

Oprah Winfrey is a well-known example of rags to riches or the triumph of the underdog. After a childhood of poverty and abuse, she moved to Nashville in her teens to live with her father, who provided direction and encouraged academic rigor, qualities that helped her find her way, set visionary goals, and become a business/media icon and philanthropist with a $3 billion fortune.[6] Another example is John Paul DeJoria of the Paul Mitchell hair care system and the Patrón Spirits Company. Growing up in a modest home in an immigrant-filled Los Angeles neighborhood, DeJoria was homeless twice before starting Paul Mitchell with $700. He sold products door to door, eventually growing the business into a "$900 million-a-year hair care heavyweight."[7] The odds in such stories are never in favor of the main characters. They enjoy no privileged backgrounds or early windfalls. Like Oprah and DeJoria, however, they overcome seemingly insurmountable challenges, surviving many bumps and bruises along the way to arrive at an inspiring place that few with such humble beginnings ever get to. That journey makes their stories inspiring to the majority of people who hear them—if they can do it, why can't I? That's why rags-to-riches stories resonate with a wide range of audiences.

Rebirth

Perhaps the best-known rebirth story is the resurrection of Jesus Christ. A rebirth story, however, need not limit itself to a physical death. In fact, in his book *The Seven Basic Plots*, author Christopher Booker uses the story of Sleeping Beauty to expand the definition of rebirth. "A hero or heroine falls under a dark spell which eventually traps them in some wintry state, akin to living death: physical or spiritual imprisonment, sleep sickness, or some other form of enchantment. For a long time, they languish in this frozen condition. Then a miraculous act of *redemption* takes place, focused on a particular figure who helps to liberate the hero or heroine from imprisonment. From the depths of darkness they are brought up into glorious light."[8] The concept of redemption is key here. Put another way, a rebirth story is about having a second chance. In business, this often takes the form of a turnaround.

Richard Teerlink helped turn Harley-Davidson around in the 1980s and '90s.[9] Before the management buyout in the early '80s, the once-iconic motorcycle company had "an operation that looked like it was sinking into the sunset," said a Dean Witter Reynolds industry analyst at the time. "The legendary but antiquated bike had become the laughingstock of the industry," reporter Scott Bieber noted.[10] Inducted into the AMA Motorcycle Hall of Fame in 2015, Teerlink was credited for "rebuild[ing] and rebrand[ing] the iconic company, establishing a new mission and new values, objectives and strategies."[11] At the onset of the rescue effort, Teerlink made it clear to investors that the company's brand was its main asset.[12] He understood that the core appeal of a Harley was not the machine itself: rather, it was the "lifestyle, an emotional attachment. That's what we have to keep marketing to." Stories of such rebirth abound in the business world and tend to be crowd-pleasers, with beating-the-odds elements similar to those of rags to riches or underdog narratives.

Overcoming the Monster

Not necessarily in the fashion of Darth Vader, *Jaws*, or the beast with jagged teeth under the bed, the "monster" in this kind of story can be any overt or covert entity or situation that can threaten survival of some sort or thwart someone from reaching an important goal. The monster could even be invisible. Think about King George VI, who overcame his monster of a speech impediment to deliver powerful, hope-inspiring addresses to his Commonwealth subjects during World War II, as depicted in the award-winning film *The King's Speech*. Often when overcoming the monster, an unsuspecting, reluctant lead character is pushed to confront the opposing force. In the Bible, Moses ran away initially from God's call for him to lead his people out of Egypt. In *Star Wars*, Luke Skywalker did not want to be bothered with taking on the evil empire until his family was murdered by Storm Troopers.

Facing a very real monster in the shape of illness, actress and photographer Kris Carr asked herself repeatedly, "How could I live with cancer without thinking of dying every day?"[1] Carr starred in two popular Budweiser Super Bowl commercials in the early 2000s and was enjoying a glamorous lifestyle when she was diagnosed with a rare form of cancer in 2003. "When first diagnosed, Carr viewed cancer as a freight train to death; now she views it as a 'catalyst' for change. She changed her lifestyle, met a new community of women, and ditched acting for writing, something she never believed she could do," journalist Lisa Stein wrote for *Scientific American*. While her doctors advised her to "watch and wait," she elected to "watch and live." Carr declared, "I'm not waiting, putting my life on hold. I'm living my life" and, in turn, encouraged others to do the same. Today, Carr is living, thriving (with cancer), publishing books, and promoting wellness to audiences far and wide.

Sometimes it can be not just an individual but a group of people or even an entire organization striving to defeat the monster. In 2015, Greenpeace Switzerland and Pure Earth released their tenth annual report titled *The World's Worst Pollution Problems*.[14] According to the report, "Pollution kills almost nine million people worldwide every year; 8.4 million of those lived in the developing world—that's 35 per cent more than deaths from smoking, almost three times more deaths than malaria."[15] To combat this deadly trend, banks like HSBC financed an innovative water filtering system to clean water waste in the Philippines, and governments such as that of Mexico worked with industries and universities to clean up sites like an old contaminated oil-refinery and turn them into public parks that draw millions of visitors a year. One article summarized the joint effort's impact: "Pollution problems can only be solved by organisations joining forces and bringing in what they are best at. . . . These are stories proving we are on the right track, and moving forward. But we need to do more with industrialisation in full swing around the world."[16]

Fighting to survive or thrive is elemental to human nature. So audiences of any type will root for defeat of the monster, whether at the hands of an individual, group, or organization, making this kind of story compelling in business and leadership stories.

The Quest

Unlike stories of rags to riches, rebirth, and overcoming the monster, which typically start from a point at which the main character's life is in bad shape, protagonists in quest stories tend to be enjoying a good life at the outset. But they are not content to sit at home, like many of us would in their situation. Instead, they know that somewhere, in a remote and possibly dangerous place, lies a prize of immeasurable value. Against his better judgment and his friends' and family's advice, the hero in this kind of story ventures out on a quest to claim this prize. The Indiana Jones movie franchise is a great example of this kind of story, where the intrepid archaeologist-adventurer played by Harrison Ford risks it all repeatedly to go after the lost Ark of the Covenant, a mystical stone, and the Holy Grail.

But real-life heroes on quests are often more inspiring. Meet former astronaut and NASA climate scientist Piers Sellers. In January 2016, at the age of sixty-one, having lived a rich, rewarding life, he was diagnosed with stage 4 pancreatic cancer and doctors told him he would have about a year and a half left to live. Instead of lamenting this turn of events or hanging out on a beach, Sellers chose to spend his last days finding ways to slow down climate change. Perhaps that is not surprising, as Sellers's whole life seemed to have revolved around the earth. A UK native, he moved to the US for post-doctoral work. Working for NASA, he eventually become a US citizen and was accepted into the space corps.

After ending his astronaut career with three space missions,

Sellers opted for a role in NASA's climate science division, leading 1500 scientists and engineers. A congressman publicly mocked his visit with Sellers because they disagreed on climate-change issues. Unwilling to back down, Sellers shot back publicly, writing a scathing op-ed piece in the *New York Times*, despite the fact that Congress funds the agency he worked for! Up until his passing on December 23, 2016, he continued to dedicate his fast-dwindling time to climate science. Like his achievements, his take on his chances of making a difference in this large-scale quest is inspiring: "We've done it before so many times. When we're in a fix, we've found a way out."[17]

Quest stories abound in business, too. James Dyson went through over five thousand prototypes of his cyclone-based vacuum cleaner before he developed the first successful model. Still, no manufacturing company in the US and UK was initially willing to license his product.[18] Today, Dyson the company returns over $500 million in annual profits and employs nearly seven thousand people worldwide. Had the founder given up on his quest for a "bagless" vacuum cleaner, Dyson would be just another name.

Almost everyone in your audience will appreciate the meaning of a quest, so think about ways to use such stories to your advantage.

SEEK THE "RIGHT" EMOTIONAL IMPACT

As suggested in the descriptions above, each of these plots has a unique emotional quality. The origin story addresses the desire to connect the dots between past and present, in an inspiring way. Rags to riches evokes empathy and gets audiences cheering for the down-on-their-luck main characters. A rebirth story is about redemption, a second chance to reverse a bad situation and evoke optimism. "overcoming the monster" stories can induce righteous anger and compel people to act to ward off a present or imminent threat. And a quest can provoke restlessness, the desire to achieve more than what life seems to promise.

Though the primary emotional qualities involved may be different, consistent across these five plots is the offer of *hope*. Bestselling novelist Harlan Coben offered the following observation about hope in a *Freakonomics* podcast interview: "[H]ope can crush your heart like an eggshell, or it can make it soar." [19] When you treat your stories and your audiences with respect and care, you can make their hearts soar.

And remember: your story can include multiple plot types. Rags to riches and origin stories often overlap, for example. Quests typically have elements of overcoming the monster. When considering what story to use, ask yourself "What do I hope to make the audience feel?" That's a critical question.

NOW IT'S YOUR TURN!

Telling stories is like riding a bike. You will not learn how just by reading about it or watching others do it: you have to saddle up and do it yourself.

So here is the process. First, write the "ugly first draft." Don't worry about what plot might fit your story best. Just write everything down, with as much detail as possible. Then, leave that first draft alone for a day or two. [20] When you come back to the draft, revise your story using the Key Elements of Storytelling discussed in chapter 1. Then, leave it alone for another day. [21] Read your draft again. This time, resist the temptation to edit, except to add important details or insights you see you've left out. When you get through all that, ask yourself the three following questions:

What is this story about?

Recall from chapter 1 that merely recounting events is not storytelling. Knowing what your story is about will give you these advantages:

1. **Theme:** What your story is about at its core becomes the theme, the spine of your story, the y-axis in its graph. For example, in all the examples Kurt Vonnegut used, fortune is the main theme. You can also apply the concept of theme to

something more specific. For example, empowering customer-services representatives to solve problems proactively, increasing awareness of who is most affected by pollution impact, or enhancing return on investments in a zero–interest-rate environment are just a few possibilities.

2. **Filter:** Knowing the spine of your story provides a critical filter to help you discard details that do not move the story forward. It's like having a nice, big, sharp pair of scissors to cut out excess. Screenwriting guru Robert McKee advises: "Creativity means creative choices of inclusion and exclusion."[22] I'd add emphasis on the latter: cut ruthlessly if you must.

3. **Plot**: It will help you decide which of the five business plots might fit your story best (more on that in a bit).

What kind of audience will find this story resonant?

If the previous question—What is this story about?—represents a top-down approach, then the question of what audience the story will resonate most with is a bottom-up one. Ultimately, storytelling in business settings is about creating fit: that between story and audience. You might have what you think is the world's greatest story, but most audience members of a certain type may disagree. Conversely, you could have what you deem to be a mundane, uninspiring story, but it may resonate deeply with some audiences. So part of your job is to think through the critical components of your story—plot, emotional quality, takeaway—and align these with what you know about your target audiences.

How has the lead character (you, in many cases) or situation changed as a result of what happens in the story?

In this stage, you can begin to think about which business plot best serves your story. It can be challenging, though, to make sense of life's seemingly random events. If you find yourself avoiding the writing, consider using one or more of the story outlines I've designed around the five business plots (see next section). Remember: change is the soul of story. In each of the plots, the lead character experiences a transformation of some kind. As a reminder, here are the specific changes associated with each plot:

- **Origin:** The present is better understood by knowing the past.
- **Rags to Riches:** The character's situation changes from very bad to very good.
- **Rebirth:** A literal or figurative near-death situation is the genesis of positive change.
- **Overcoming the Monster:** Something bad or evil gets eliminated.
- **Quest:** A seemingly unachievable goal is achieved.

What if your story fits more than one of these plots? It is ultimately your choice whether you follow any one of the plots or some combination, based on the outlines below. Think of them not as rigid rules but as guidelines and sources of inspiration for your story-mining and -writing process. But definitely consider using one or more of the outlines to get your process started; that's what they're for!

THE FIVE BASIC PLOTS IN BUSINESS COMMUNICATION: OUTLINES TO EXPEDITE YOUR STORYTELLING

In the following pages, you will find a basic outline and an example loosely based on real life to go with each plot. (These examples are not actual first-person stories—except for the story about me. I've created them using known facts about the people in question to demonstrate how to use each type of plot.) Use these outlines to help you jump-start your draft. As you develop your story, you can work to make each transition seamless and make each story unique by filling in its particular details.

ORIGIN STORY OUTLINE

_____ (business/career) started when _____ (interesting challenge, opportunity, or connection between two previously unrelated ideas).

Because _____ (I/we) realized _____ (how you decided this idea was big enough to be a business/that this opportunity fit your vocation).

This idea grabbed (me/us) because _____ (how the idea combined with your own internal drive/came at just the right time).

With the help of _____ (people or resources), _____ (company's initial launch/stabilizing your career).

At first, _____ (problems).

But then, _____ (solutions).

Today, _____ no longer _____ (what has changed since the point of origin).

But the same _____ (vision that guided you initially) now _____ (how that vision continues to shape your company/career today).

And that's why _____ (application to audience).

ORIGIN STORY:
AIRBNB[23]

Our business **started when** my roommate and I couldn't pay our rent. We decided to create a website posting space in our apartment—three air mattresses on the living room floor—as available to rent for the weekend. This was the same weekend a big convention was in town and all the hotels were full, so we easily got three people to stay with us.

At the time, renting those air mattresses was what we needed to do to get by. But **because** of the overwhelming response we received, we **realized** we were on to something bigger. **The idea grabbed** my roommate and me **because** we both wanted to get away from designing "stuff" we thought people might not even need.

With the help of a tech-savvy friend, we launched an official website for our company. We got an extra boost from a huge event in town (creating more demand for housing than the local hotels could meet). We had tons of people share their space and tons of people booking those spaces.

At first, we had a great idea but no money. **But then** we realized that if we handled the most awkward part of the transaction—the money—guests and hosts would be willing to pay us a transaction fee. We ran into further snags when a host had a guest destroy her apartment. We apologized publicly and immediately provided substantial insurance for hosts.

Today, our business **no longer** works out of that same apartment where three people first rented our air mattresses. **But the same** value we place on experiences rather than "stuff" keeps bringing people to our web platform and keeps urging us to make people's experience of renting each others' homes safer and more meaningful.

And that's why we want to see the sharing economy thrive and believe that this new investment opportunity is worth pursuing.

RAGS TO RICHES OUTLINE

This year, _____ (current level of success). But it wasn't always like this.

In fact, _____ (where you were when your company/career began—or further back to childhood if applicable).

But even then, _____ (personal qualities/people who intervened/lessons that guided you).

Finally, _____ (how you got the chance that led to the "riches").

Just when it looked like _____ (possible success), _____ (I/we) still _____ (further setbacks). But _____ (I/we) kept _____ (your response to the setbacks).

After _____ (sum up past struggles) _____ (success). That was when (I/we) felt like (I/we) had made it.

And when I look back, _____ (how the "rags" make you think about "riches").

RAGS TO RICHES:
JOHN PAUL DEJORIA[24]

This year, I made *Forbes* magazine's list of the world's billionaires. My hair care company brings in $900 million each year. My tequila company turned a once-derided liquor into a luxury item.

But it wasn't always like this.

In fact, I've been homeless twice. When my first wife left me with my young son, I collected bottles and cans for spare change while I looked for a job. Later on, when I was about to launch my hair care company, my second wife and I split up and I slept in my car for a while. I was expecting that to be temporary because my business partner and I had a backer who'd promised to give us $500,000. But it never came through.

But even then, I knew how to work hard and had no problem selling things door-to-door. As a nine-year-old, I'd sold Christmas cards door-to-door. At ten, I was getting up at 4 a.m. for a paper route. Then I sold encyclopedias door-to-door. I knew what it was like to face rejection and keep a smile on my face at the next person's door. I had to keep being hopeful, no matter the number of rejections. And to sell hair care products, I just went from one salon to the next.

Finally, people began buying our products.

Just when it looked like we were starting to make it, I *still* had trouble paying our bills. We'd started out with so little—$700 between my co-founder and myself! **But** we **kept** knocking on doors and refusing to give up our optimism that our product was different and was going to catch on.

After a couple of years of real struggle, we were able to pay our bills, and my partner and I had money to take home, a couple of thousand dollars apiece. **That was when we felt like we'd made it.**

And when I look back, those difficult years, those years when hope was all I had, have made me want to give others hope.

REBIRTH (TURNAROUND) OUTLINE

_____ was in a hopeless situation because _____.

I am now _____ because _____ (circumstantial reasons). What drove me was _____ (intrinsic motivation).

Eventually, I secured the much needed _____ (key ingredient in turnaround).

That's when _____.

From that point on, _____. Even with _____ (further challenges), I was able to _____ with _____ (other people and resources.)

Anyone can _____, but I _____ (different from usual mindset/behaviors).

Even with all the _____ (successes,) what I am most proud of is _____.

_____ wouldn't be here today if it weren't for _____.

REBIRTH (TURNAROUND):
SALLIE KRAWCHECK[25]

I **was in a hopeless situation because** in my twenties I kept moving from one career to another, unable to find the right fit.

I am now the chair of an 80,000-member network of women in finance **because** my thirtieth birthday was coming up and I felt so old. I was looking for something more solid, a career trajectory that I could follow for the rest of my life. **What drove me was** a feeling that unless I did that, all my education was going to go to waste as I hopped from one career to another.

Eventually I secured the much-needed "aha moment" I had been waiting for. It hit me: "I should be a research analyst."

That's when I realized how I could put my interests and education to use.

From that point on, it was just a matter of acting on my plan to become a research analyst. **Even with** many career shifts ahead—leading large, complex businesses as CFO at Citi Group, being publicly fired from two firms, and now, in my fifties, becoming an entrepreneur—**I was able to** stay focused on research, **with** the good fortune early in my career of landing at Bernstein, where a diversity of voices mattered and people were too focused on results to get sidetracked by the fact that I was a woman in the "man's world" of finance.

Anyone can put their interests and education to use, **but I** was committed to lifelong learning, and pushed myself to find jobs where I would have to learn a lot.

Even with my high-profile work in the financial sector, **what I am most proud of is** finding meaningful work—work that puts my skills to use and that matters to me.

I **wouldn't be here today if it weren't for** that moment at the end of my twenties, standing in my kitchen, when it clicked that I wanted to be a research analyst.

OVERCOMING THE MONSTER OUTLINE

_____ (Time and place) I was _____. (Describe a normal day in the life. Introduce the characters.)

One day, _____. (An unexpected and overwhelming challenge landed on your lap.)

At first, I was _____. (How you were lost and resisted to meet the challenge.)

Then, _____. (Something happened or someone you met was about to change your mind).

So, I decided to _____. (A deliberate moment when you tackled the "monster" head on.)

Then, _____. (The beginning of your journey of overcoming the monster.)

Despite my best efforts, _____. (Setbacks and rebounds.)

Finally, when _____. (Final "battle" with the monster. Peace ensued. A new state emerged.)

I realize now _____. (What you learned from this journey.)

In fact, _____. (Reasons your story is relevant to your audience.)

OVERCOMING THE MONSTER:
KRIS CARR[26]

It was February 2003 and **I was** returning home to New York City after partying at a film festival. I was thirty-one years old, and the film-festival partying was just another part of my fast-paced life as an actress and photographer.

But **one day**, the morning after I got home, I felt tired and sore. By the end of the day, I wasn't just sore—I also had painful abdominal cramps and could hardly catch my breath. I phoned my doctor and went to see him the next day. A few days later, I was diagnosed with a rare form of cancer.

At first, I was shocked and angry, overwhelmed by the question of how to live a normal life while battling cancer. **Then** my doctor suggested that I focus on strengthening my immune system. **So, I decided to** make myself an expert on healing.

Then I read everything I could about cancer. I became vegan. I surrounded myself with other young women who had cancer too. I started filming the whole journey. And I started interviewing doctors as if they were applying for the "job" of saving me.

Despite my best efforts, one of the doctors I "interviewed" told me I would need a triple-organ transplant.

Finally, when I found the doctor currently treating me, I placed my trust in a skilled oncologist who believes I can live a full life with this cancer, and I don't have to pursue chemo or radiation immediately, let alone a triple organ transplant!

I realize now that I want to live the fullest, healthiest life possible. **In fact,** I believe anyone diagnosed with any disease should focus on *living*. I want to help you have the same perspective.

THE QUEST OUTLINE[27]

I want _____ .

I want it because _____ . (Your backstory. Introduce main characters, set the hook.)

To get it, I _____ (action).

However, something got in my way: _____ . (Your journey of overcoming obstacles and challenges to get what you want.)

All the time, I was thinking that _____ . (The assumption you had or the worldviews you held in the beginning of your journey.)

The turning point came when _____ . (A breakthrough moment when you realized you had to change your assumptions.)

When that happened, I realized _____ . (The main learning point for you in this story.)

After that, I _____ . (What you did as a result of your realization.)

What I also realize now is that _____ . (Reasons your story is relevant to your audience.)

THE QUEST:
ESTHER CHOY (ME!)

I want everyone to enjoy hearing a dry and technical presentation as if they were listening to a tantalizing story. It sounds crazy, but it's not impossible.

I want it because I experienced the power of story when I worked as an admissions officer for a top-tier business school, and had to read thousands of essays. Many were uninspiring, technical, and dry. Occasionally, I came across essays that told stories and were so well written that I lost track of time when I read them. And the applicants who wrote these essays were more likely to be admitted than those who could not tell good stories, as long as they had strong credentials. Then it got me wondering: Does telling good stories only work in competitive admissions? The answer, I believed, was a definite no!

To get what I wanted, **I** got my own MBA and founded a company called Leadership Story Lab to teach and consult on leadership storytelling.

However, something got in my way. Even though most people find storytelling in business intuitive and appealing, they don't necessarily value it enough to *pay* for it.

All the time, I was thinking that "if you build it, they will come." I couldn't have been more wrong.

The turning point came when I thought back to where I'd started: admissions. Interest in storytelling alone is not going to get potential clients to hire help. They need an imminent deadline, application due date, product launch, funding deadline, or something similar that causes urgency.

When that happened, I realized that my marketing (or lack thereof) was all off.

After that, I understood that timing and targeting are crucial. I need to offer my expertise to those who understand the intrinsic values of storytelling in business *and* have an immediate and high-stakes reason to apply this valuable skill set.

What I also realize now is that just because I have a great idea and others agree with me, it does not mean that it will translate into a business opportunity. I need to proactively find the audiences with an urgent need for what I offer. And that's what I've tried to do.

We have covered a lot of ground here, from how you can plot the movement of story on a graph, to the Five Basic Business Story Plots, their distinctive emotional appeals, and outlines to jump-start your own stories. I hope you're beginning to see how you can integrate these tools and build your story so that it resonates as deeply as possible with your target audiences. Even on days when you do not feel creative or inspired, you can still craft compelling stories when you practice using these tools and, ideally, make their use second nature.

In the next section of the book, we will explore in detail how to bring stories to life. The first step is to make a connection with your audience through point of view.

part

TWO

BRINGING STORIES TO LIFE

CHAPTER 3

LOOK WHO'S LISTENING

THIS CHAPTER IS ABOUT point of view—specifically, how to understand and harness your audience's point of view to tell more powerful stories. The best way to illustrate the concept of point of view is, not surprisingly, with a story. Below you'll read one you may have heard before, but probably not in the same way you'll hear it this time.

THE TRUE STORY OF THE THREE LITTLE PIGS

Surely you've heard the classic story "The Three Little Pigs"—the tale of three sibling pigs who built houses of straw, sticks, and bricks. Recall that a big bad wolf came along, blew down the houses of straw and sticks, and ate up two of the three pigs. Only the brick-house-owning pig escaped, thanks to the sturdiness of his home.

But what if there was more to the story? Have you heard the story of the "Big Badly Misunderstood Wolf?" That alternate title could represent author Jon Scieszka's take on the story of the three little pigs, or what he calls *The True Story of the Three Little Pigs*, his picture book.[1] He rewrote the famous narrative from a very different point of view: the wolf's. And that changes the story's tone, meaning, and takeaways dramatically.

First, the "Big Bad Wolf" has a name: Alexander T. Wolf, but people call him Al. From his jail cell, Al narrates what actually happened that fateful day with the three pigs many years ago. "Nobody knows the real story," he says, "because nobody has ever heard my side of the story."

It all started with a cup of sugar, a cold, and a big sneeze. Back then, Al was a young strapping wolf, and one day he wanted to make a birthday cake for his grandmother, even though he had a terrible cold. But he ran out of sugar. Just like most of us might, Al walked down the street to borrow the sugar from one of his neighbors.

Guess who his neighbors were?

Yes, the three pigs, who happened to be brothers. According to Al, two of them were not very smart but one was, which explains the choices of straw, sticks, and bricks as house-building materials. When Al knocked on the door of the nearest neighbor—the pig in the house of straw—no one answered. He knocked again, but still no answer. All of a sudden, Al was overcome by an irresistible urge to sneeze. He did, powerfully enough that the whole house crashed down, leaving the pig lying at the bottom of a big pile of straw. Dead. Al thought it would be such a terrible waste to let a perfectly good stack of bacon go to waste. So he ate it, and went on to the next house, still in search of sugar. And we know how it ends.

Point of view is everything. Note that in both the original story and Scieszka's alternative version, the characters, sequence of events, and ending are identical. There were three brothers, a wolf, three houses built of very different materials, a request to be let in, and a massive rush of air that destroyed two of the homes. And of course there were two dead pigs.

Hearing the new rendition of the old story, however, you get a very different picture of the "Big Bad Wolf." He's not so bad after all. You might even feel bad for him because he was only trying to be a good grandson by making a birthday cake for his grandmother. And all that huffing and puffing was the result of the cold. The eating of the pigs was arguably a good ecological practice, as Al didn't want the food to go to waste!

As this example suggests, what you include and exclude may produce a very different story from that of someone else, even if the characters and events were the same. That leads us to a critical point: Telling a story with a strategic point of view is not about starting only from what you know. Rather, it is about first being clear with what you are trying to accomplish—pitching an idea, suggesting a change, winning an account, or whatever—and then crafting your story from the point of view that will be most persuasive to those you need to convince. You have to take yourself out of your own mindset, preferences, and biases and put yourself into the shoes of your most important audience, asking "What do they **want** to know? What do they **need** to know?"

In the following example, a Chicago company has its roots in the 9/11 tragedy. This fact is important to the couple who started the company, but not (as we will see) relevant or helpful to the customers of that company.

AN ENTREPRENEUR'S INSPIRATION MAY NOT INSPIRE HIS CUSTOMERS

On September 11, 2001, Gregoire Klees-Johnson's wife Kristine decided to take a day off from work in New York City. The couple had just adopted a puppy and Kristine wanted to stay home during the puppy's first few days in their New Jersey apartment, which was on the Hudson River just across from the twin World Trade Center towers. That morning, as Gregoire was already on his way to work in New Jersey as a competitive intelligence analyst, Kristine watched from her front window as the unimaginable happened in Manhattan: two planes struck the Twin Towers and the burning buildings collapsed to the ground. Kristine normally took the subway and exited at the World Trade Center stop every day. If not for the new puppy, Kristine (a schoolteacher) would've been working very close to the Twin Towers, her survival in the hands of fate.

The couple's outlook on life changed completely that day. They thought about what mattered most to them, then decided to move back to Chicago, their previous home, and start an early childhood-enrichment company called Bubbles Academy. Having unwanted front-row seats to one of the most tragic events in US history motivated Gregoire and Kristine to uproot themselves, change their career paths, and take on the financial risks of entrepreneurs. It was Bubbles Academy's reason for its existence. Such was the founders' story that Gregoire sought to refine ten years post-9/11, when I met him at one of my workshops.

The more we studied his target customers, however, the more dissonant the story seemed from their perspective. The majority of them were stay-at-home mothers with one young child. They were city dwellers, college-educated, in their late 20s and early 30s. They were no more or less patriotic than the average American. Importantly, they often felt isolated and overwhelmed by motherhood. They constantly questioned whether they were doing the right things for their children, if they were giving them all that they could.

For this audience, being reminded of 9/11 would be discordant with the benefits Bubbles Academy hoped to deliver. At best it might be distracting; at worst it might cause them even more stress and turn them off from the business. At first it was difficult for Gregoire to accept this feedback, as he'd thought about Bubbles Academy's origin story for a long time and remembered that fateful day in 2001 vividly. But in the end, his empathy for customers and desire to build a successful business motivated him to change his story. His new founders' story downplayed what their audience didn't want or need to know: the traumatic origin of the happy, upbeat, positive, and inspiring early-childhood-education business. Instead, the story played up what the audience wanted and needed to know: Kristine's expertise in education, Gregoire's family history in the arts and creative business, and the couple's passion for early childhood development. It went over very well.

The next example involves another domain: investment pitch books for institutional investor clients or prospects, such as pension funds. Once again, this example shows that your story has to answer your audience's questions—and if it doesn't, you will lose that audience.

PEOPLE DON'T CARE HOW MUCH YOU KNOW UNTIL THEY KNOW HOW MUCH YOU CARE

If you've seen one investment pitch book, you've pretty much seen all of them: glossy and professional-looking, with a sharp focus on touting the value of the investment firm's history, philosophy, and process, along with organization charts and the impeccable experience the people at each position in those charts have, and detailed data-heavy valuation models that drive truly outstanding performance. One way to describe these pitch books: It's all about ME!

One real estate investment trust hedge fund's old pitch book used to be just like that. The fund, based in Chicago, invests opportunistically in global real estate securities funds, or real estate investment trusts (REITS). Structured as a hedge fund, it can take both long and short positions, enabling its fund managers to invest flexibly in globally listed real estate stocks. The valuation process, as you might imagine, is extremely analytical and quantitative. The firm also uses a "bottom-up" valuation approach, identifying investments on a stock-by-stock basis rather than a macro investing approach driven by a certain view of a country, sector, or other big-picture variables like interest rates, political events/trends, and others. Finally, the fund is often contrarian in its philosophy, going against what peer businesses might do or believe—a quality that appeals to many investors looking for a competitive edge.

Having worked with several other investment funds, I knew that all of them considered themselves contrarians. The question, then, for any given firm is whether prospective clients believe them. The answer in my client firm's case was no. Despite its strong average annualized return of 22% for eleven years straight, its fund managers had a very hard time raising more assets to manage. So the managers decided that it was time to change their approach from me-centric to much more client-focused.

But how?

After I went over their pitch book, a central problem with the pitch book emerged immediately. In the older version, every slide was essentially aimed at answering the same question: "We are SO good, why wouldn't any client want to invest with us?" As you can see, this approach was rather self-centered, even if the pitch book was following industry presentation protocol.

More importantly, we outlined the questions prospective clients actually wanted answers to, including "How did the fund have such stellar performance for so long?" and "Can the team continue its track record?" Imagine that a friend recommended a restaurant with three Michelin stars where she'd had a wonderful meal the previous week, but you felt doubtful. In fact, as it turns out in this slightly fictionalized world, many Michelin-starred restaurants lose their head chef, sous chefs, and dessert chef soon after they achieve three-star status, as these now more valuable professionals are wooed away by competitor establishments. Beyond that, even a highly rated restaurant with its original staff intact could have an off night for any number of reasons. So, although this particular restaurant came highly recommended, you couldn't be sure you would have the same stellar experience your friend had. In the same way, many institutional investors are justified in being skeptical when fund managers make a pitch for their business.

Knowing what questions the pitch book should be answering—as driven by prospects' natural skepticism—won us the first half of the battle. Whereas the approach had been "Hey, we have something really awesome to sell you," the more strategic approach after our deliberation was "We are a thought leader in REIT investments. Allow us to walk you through the essence of REITs and how to invest in these so you can deliver greater investment returns for your fund and clients."

With the right questions as a guide, the new and improved pitch book's content no longer centers on the firm itself, but on how the fund can sustain its strong past performance going forward. So, instead of just repeating over and over how great the fund and the fund managers are, my client's new pitch book aims to communicate how the investment firm has been able to achieve these results and how they are repeatable. Thus, we won the first half of the battle by understanding that we had to move from explaining the *whats* (what makes us great) over and over to providing audiences a complete tour of the *hows* (how we deliver strong returns).

We won the second half of the battle by creating pitch-book content that did just that: explaining the hows, using stories from the categories discussed in chapter 2. These brief narratives include how the fund got started (origin story), what it set out to achieve (quest) given the cyclicality of the real estate market, how it fared (very well compared to other funds) during the Global Financial Crisis (rebirth), and how it continues to outperform its benchmarks despite low interest rates and global political uncertainty (overcoming the monster). The success of the new pitch book lies in having created a presentation that is meant to be delivered in person, to bring the stories within to life, rather than representing a more static document that a prospect could read on their own and struggle to differentiate from myriad others in the industry. The new pitch book worked so well that within about eighteen months the fund had surpassed its asset-raising goal for the first time!

AIA: ACKNOWLEDGE-INSPIRE-ASPIRE IN ACTION

Remember one of our trusted tools, the Three-Act Formula, from Chapter 1? Briefly, every story should have three classical parts called the Three-Act Formula. In Act I or the beginning, the story opens with a specific scene, ushering in the main characters and planting a hook. In Act II, the storytellers take their audiences through the journey of how the main characters overcome their challenges. Then in Act III, the story reaches the final resolution and the takeaway. In crafting your story with a point of view that strongly resembles that of your audiences, you can also follow the Three-Act Formula *in principle*.

The following is an example from one of my clients, Glenn Hollister, a principal of the Evanston-based consultancy ZS Associates, and how he got a group of sales executives excited for a technological change through the use of the AIA model. In 2015,

Glenn had to present to four hundred frontline sales executives at one of the top four US airlines. The presentation featured a preview of an overhauled sales dashboard, one that all salespeople would be expected to use, but that was not yet live.

Let's face it: no one loves big changes in any setting—or at least very few of us do. That's why executives and consultants have such a hard time making change happen in their organizations. Statements like "This new technology is really going to change your work lives for the better" are met with skepticism at best, outright mutiny at worst. So Glenn knew what he was up against in trying to convince the sales executives of the new dashboard's value.

Luckily, he was armed with the AIA framework. First, he began his hour-long presentation by acknowledging his audience. He did so by describing in great detail a day in the life of an airline sales executive, literally minute by minute. He did all that before mentioning anything about the new dashboard. Wouldn't the audience be bored by that, you might ask. Not at all. The executives he spoke to were not only paying close attention to Glenn's presentation, but they were giggling, clapping, and cheering. They knew that this consulting firm could not have come up with such detail about their daily work lives without taking great care to study their processes, procedures, and (lots of) pain points. They appreciated being acknowledged.

Acknowledging your audience is like stabilizing patients in the ER. Once your audience feels acknowledged, they are much more ready to listen to what you have to offer. So after gaining their trust and attention, Glenn *inspired* his audience to envision a much more efficient way to spend their work days by unveiling the new dashboard and all its features. He walked them through the major functionalities and benefits. Then by comparing and contrasting their current day in a life (current state) with the state of affairs once the new dashboard went live (desired state), Glenn enabled his audience to picture vividly how much easier their lives would be with the new dashboard.

Finally, he got his audience to *aspire* to perform at a higher level: spending much less time on emails and prep work and more time engaging with their customers. Currently, these frontline salespeople had five major roles that demanded their time. The new dashboard

More selling time

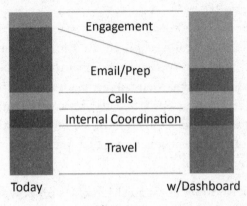

Figure 3-1

would significantly reduce the time they had to spend on email and other prep. And that freed them up to engage and re-cultivate relationships with customers.

As you can see from one of the slides that Glenn used in his presentation in Figure 3-1, he highlighted the big advantage of the dashboard: reduction of email and prep time from about half of all time spent in the current state to something like 20% in the desired state (see Figure 3-1).

You too can follow the AIA model for any presentation, pitch, or other form of persuasion. First, acknowledge your audiences by telling stories from their point of view. Second, inspire them to feel good about your proposed changes, ideas, products, or services. Third, get them to aspire to a different future with concrete details, one with you and your solution as important parts of it.

LOOK WHO'S LISTENING EXERCISE

Being truly fluent in more than one language means that you can switch back and forth between them with ease. The same is true with point of view. Yet mastering point of view, just like learning multiple languages, takes time and concerted practice. So how do you become fluent with point of view? How do you put yourself effectively in others' shoes? The best exercise to make that happen is the "Look Who's Listening" approach.

To describe this approach, I'll use a real example from 2014, when a large bank (U.S. Bank) acquired the Chicagoland branches of a smaller bank (Charter One Bank). As shown below, U.S. Bank, Charter Bank, and Charter Bank's customers each had a different point of view of the acquisition. For U.S. Bank, the acquisition meant growth; for Charter Bank, the acquisition reflected focus. And for Charter Bank's customers, the acquisition meant uncertainty.[2]

1. U.S. Bank Announces Acquisition to Its Employees.

The Charter One acquisition is a defining moment for U.S. Bank. It defines us as a major player in deposit banking, making us one of the top ten deposit banks in Chicago.[3] And, with over 3,000 branch locations, we are now one of the nation's top five banks by number of branches.[4]

In purchasing Charter One, we have added nearly 100 branch locations in Chicagoland. That means we now have over 150 branches in the Chicago area. And that, in turn, means our local deposit market share has almost doubled.[5]

But as we grow, we will not allow our vision to be lost or redefined. We want to help consumers and businesses achieve their financial goals. We will continue to invest in communities. And we will start our commitment to the community by offering each employee from Charter One a similar job—either at the same branch or transferred to another branch.[6] First and foremost, we will remain mindful that this acquisition simply gives us more communities to be part of.

2. Charter One Announces U.S. Bank Buyout to Its Customers.

Today we have reached an agreement with U.S. Bank. After long and careful consideration, we have decided to pursue the best future for Charter One by focusing on where we are strongest and where we see the most opportunity for growth.

We believe U.S. Bank will do everything in their power to provide a positive future for their new customers and our former Chicagoland employees.

We also firmly believe that we still have a future in Chicago ourselves. This future lies in lending. Our agreement with U.S. Bank allows us to make this future possible.[7]

3. Former Charter One Customers Respond to the Change

This week, customers of Charter One learned that their local branches will soon become U.S. Bank branches. Notification letters went out to all Charter One customers, assuring them that their accounts would not change and no new fees would be added. But this addressed just one concern among many.

"When I became a Charter One customer," says a customer from Chicago's Wicker Park neighborhood, "it was because I wanted a bank with a neighborhood feel. One where I would know the tellers and they would know me. A bank that didn't try to sell me something each time I walked through the door. How can U.S. Bank preserve this personality? They're one of the biggest banks in the country."

A customer from North Lawndale expressed particular concern for his lower-income neighborhood. "Mergers and acquisitions mean one thing for low-income communities: closures. And low-income households depend on being able to go to a branch location close by.[8] They can't pay to ride the CTA every time they need to make a transaction. We would like some assurance from U.S Bank that they don't plan to close branches in North Lawndale, but so far we haven't heard anything."

If you were on the communication team at U.S. Bank, how would you handle interactions with your Charter One Bank counterpart and the customers you're inheriting from that bank?

Below, I'll provide three general steps to use point of view in the most strategic way to address this challenge. Then we'll walk through how U.S. Bank can structure its communications more effectively for its key audiences, using the three-step model.

STEP 1:

Describe audience, write script, sketch current/desired states

- Describe the people (or person) you are persuading in as much detail as possible.
- Write the "script" you are using to persuade them, without necessarily thinking from their point of view.
- Sketch out the current state and desired state as you see them.

STEP 2:

List what's known and unknown; draw a Venn diagram

- List everything you know about the impending change (i.e., buyout and transition in this case).
- List everything you don't know about the buyout and transition (this may sound strange, but will make more sense below).
- List everything your audience already knows about the buyout and transition.
- List everything your audience doesn't know about the buyout and transition.
- Draw a Venn diagram of what you know and what your audience needs and wants to know.

STEP 3:

Restructure your message based on the AIA model: Acknowledge, Inspire, and Aspire.

Now let's walk through how U.S. Bank could handle its communications about the acquisition, using the approach above.

Step 1

How would U.S. Bank describe their Charter One Bank counterparts? Here are some possibilities.

- Professional, authentic
- Place high value on customer experience

- Down-to-earth, exemplifying idea of "citizens helping citizens"
- Busy: often have a line of customers at their branches

How would U.S. Bank describe the customers they are about to inherit from Charter One?

- Lead hectic lives
- Like interactions to be helpful and courteous (not just quick); respond to a welcoming, hospitable presence
- Appreciate "the city of neighborhoods"—like to be remembered by name at local bank
- Don't "suffer fools gladly"

Now write the "script" to communicate with Charter One counterparts based on the ideas above. A basic version could be something like:

> Effective immediately, due to U.S. Bank's purchase of Charter One's Chicagoland locations, we will be transitioning your location to a U.S. Bank branch.
>
> We are offering employment packages and transfers to all of our customer-facing employees. We will also ensure that key U.S. Bank staff are in place to help navigate changes.
>
> We appreciate your role in this transition.

Last, sketch the picture of current and desired state for Charter One Bank counterparts and customers; examples below.

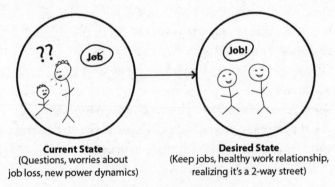

Current State
(Questions, worries about
job loss, new power dynamics)

Desired State
(Keep jobs, healthy work relationship,
realizing it's a 2-way street)

Figure 3-2: Current/desired state for counterparts

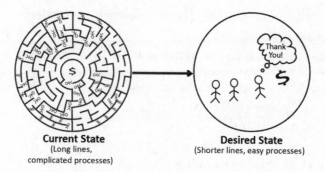

Current State
(Long lines,
complicated processes)

Desired State
(Shorter lines, easy processes)

Figure 3-3: Current/desired state for customers

Step 2

First, list everything you know about the buyout and transition for Charter One.

- Competitive employment packages offered to Charter One employees
- U.S. Bank C-suite objectives and shareholder interests
- Strengths and weaknesses of Charter One
- Branch closings
- New branch managers

Next, list everything you *don't* know about the buyout and transition for Charter One.

- How many employees will stay long-term, especially among employees offered a transfer?
- How will Charter One employees meet the challenges of implementing changes to meet U.S. Bank C-suite and shareholder objectives?
- How eager will these employees be to work on Charter One weaknesses?
- What effect will branch closings have on morale?
- What personality dynamics will exist between Charter One employees and new USB branch managers?

Now repeat the same two questions, except this time for the bank customers. List everything they already know or believe about the buyout and transition.

- What it is like to be a Charter One customer—experience with customer service, account terms, and so on
- What it is like to change banks
- The experience of having smaller companies subsumed by larger ones
- The idea that bigger corporations don't always have good customer service
- The fear that bigger corporations might be more likely to close branches
- The idea that bigger corporations can offer more amenities

Now list everything bank customers *don't* know about the buyout and transition.

- Most do not know what it's like to be a U.S. Bank customer— how their experience might actually improve from when they were Charter One customers
- U.S. Bank's plans to close branch locations
- What's in it for U.S. Bank to keep them as customers
- Who will be in charge of each branch
- Incentives offered to Charter One employees to stay (meaning the customers would see familiar faces at their branches)

Next, use the lists above to draw a Venn diagram of what you know and what your Charter One counterparts *need and want to know*, as seen in Figure 3-4.

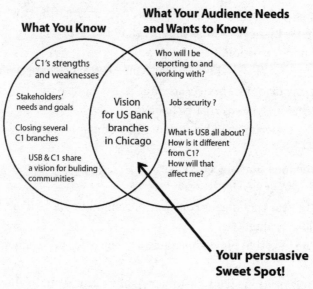

Figure 3-4

Draw a Venn diagram of what you know and what the *bank customers* need and want to know, as seen in Figure 3-5.

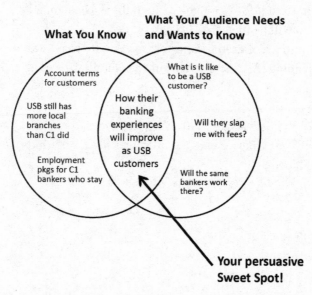

Figure 3-5

Step 3

Describe your audiences again after having gone through the analysis above. Now rewrite the "script" you would use to communicate with them, using the AIA—Acknowledge, Inspire, Aspire—approach discussed earlier in the book.

Description of *Charter One Bank Counterparts:*
- Professional and authentic
- Formal, but without being cold or condescending
- Value customer experience
- Share U.S. Bank's concern for customers
- Can be helpful to customers with transition
- Busy: often have a line of customers

Script for *Charter One Bank Counterparts:*
Charter One bankers are known in the industry and among customers as down-to-earth and customer-focused. We've seen firsthand, for example, how often Charter One's Chicagoland bankers greet customers by name.

   Like Charter One, U.S. Bank has a vision for strengthening the communities we serve. And so, as Charter One branches become U.S. Bank branches, we want to work alongside you to help consumers and businesses achieve their financial goals.

Description of *Charter One Customers:*
- Communicating with Charter One customers right at the moment the acquisition becomes public knowledge. Which traits are relevant at this moment?
- They are busy. Communication has to be brief and concise.
- They are used to the feel of a hometown bank.
- They don't suffer fools gladly. They are good at detecting "BS," so communication needs to be transparent and direct.
- They appreciate courtesy and helpfulness. So reiterate, with sincerity, how we will help with transition.
- They love the concept of "city of neighborhoods." So mention their branch location by name.

Script for Charter One Customers (from a specific branch area):

Thank you for being a loyal Charter One customer for over five years. Your loyalty has allowed Charter One to play a vital role in the financial health of Lincoln Square.

Today we are writing to announce that Charter One's Chicagoland locations are becoming U.S. Bank branches. This transition will mean further convenience and more resources for you and your neighborhood, while maintaining everything you value in your neighborhood bank.

To continue to support your community, we have offered many Charter One bankers jobs within their home branch. And we are ensuring that Charter One customers will not experience any changes to the terms of their savings or checking accounts.

Please feel free to communicate with us about your questions and financial goals. We look forward to working together to make this transition a big step forward.

For U.S. Bank, the acquisition represented 100 new branch locations in the Chicago area. But that's not what its Charter One counterparts or Charter One's customers wanted or needed to know. Through the Look Who's Listening approach, U.S. Bank can identify exactly the answers that truly matter to its audiences—answers about job security for the counterparts and small-bank service for Charter One's customers.

Incorporating your audiences' point of view in your storytelling draws you that much closer to the people you are aiming to persuade. What if the foundation of your story is a mountain of data? The next chapter shows you how to become an expert Data Storyteller, combining the strengths of each.

CHAPTER 4

TELLING STORIES WITH DATA

BIG DATA IS EVERYWHERE. Even the quickest scan of online business news will yield a barrage of articles about what companies plan to do with massive, often innovative data sets. For example, human capital management and payroll company Automatic Data Processing has tested software that could reportedly predict potential employees' likelihood of quitting based on their pay, commute distance, and a range of other factors.[1] Clear Channel Outdoor, the nation's largest billboard company, has created billboards that can be customized to drivers' interests based on data collected from hundreds of millions of cellular subscribers to AT&T and other carriers.[2]

Business isn't the only domain where data use is mounting. Like retailers, political campaigns have been using Big Data to craft and communicate key messages to target voters, especially for the 2016 presidential election. As noted in a 2016 *Forbes* article, "Depth of information means that every message issued, whether it appears on the website, in a speech, an email or through canvassing, can be something better than one-size-fits-all."[3] Big Data even has agricultural applications, as new software systems can use sensor-based information to help farmers understand the best strategies—such as seed location—for optimal crop yields.

In short, we are in a Data Boom period, with virtually every public and private domain enjoying unprecedented availability of information and data-analysis tools. Whether you are a data scientist, marketing director, policymaker, or research analyst, the accelerating volume, velocity, and variety[4] of data beg one critical question: *How are you going to communicate the meaning and implications of massive quantities of relevant information to your audience, to get them onboard with your ideas and plans?*

The answer is simple: story. Using principal storytelling elements will boost the impact of your message dramatically and prevent you and your audience from drowning in an ever-rising sea of information. This chapter is about how to use story to communicate data-rich messages most effectively, starting with understanding your audiences and what matters most to them.

THE NUMBER ONE PROBLEM: TOO MUCH DATA

Four years ago, my family and I moved into a bigger house. While the move was welcome, it also meant myriad bathroom and kitchen renovations, installation of window treatments and cabinets, repainting, and so on. The good news was that I had the help of a capable interior designer. The bad news was that we struggled to communicate. I would ask about pricing or delivery dates—for bedroom curtains, for example—and rather than answering me directly, she would offer a wealth of information that seemed irrelevant: "I went to the supplier's 'work room' and inquired about the popularity and available yardage of the fabric and they said . . . and then I spoke to the seamstress three times and she said. . . ." Sometimes I would get my answer at the end of the monologue. Sometimes I wouldn't.

As I thought more about it, I realized that this kind of communication challenge happened with lots of service providers, from auto mechanics to IT support staff. Only recently did I gain better perspective on this phenomenon, when I spoke to Greg Kim, a friend who oversees customer retention for a major online retailer, managing a team of data scientists. "You know why they do that, right?" he said when I mentioned my frustration with the verbose explanations of service providers. I ventured that some of them might have been motivated by money, as they were paid by the hour. "No," he said, "they do it to demonstrate their value." That is, they want me to know how hard they've worked, how knowledgeable they are, and how they have bent over backward to provide service to me. I, on the other hand, just wanted a direct, concise answer to my question, with the opportunity to ask probing questions if needed.

Seeing that disconnect helped me understand the challenge of making a presentation based on data: the presenters want to display just how much data they've accumulated—increasing not only their own value and credibility, but also the value and credibility of the information they are sharing. However, the audience is not impressed with a flood of data. They want to know what the data means, and why they should care.

DATA + STORY: A MODERN LEADERSHIP MODEL

In October 2015, I had the pleasure of teaching a workshop on how to deliver captivating presentations for the Advertising Research Foundation. During a break, Michael Heitner, the organization's executive VP, shared a casual observation with me that ultimately helped lay the foundation for this chapter. Heitner mentioned that he has noticed how preoccupied many professionals are with working on their projects and preparing related presentations, such that by the end of the process they are truly exhausted. In fact, they are so fatigued that they sometimes even forget they still have to deliver the actual presentation! Everything involved in the *preparation* prevents them from attending sufficiently to the *presentation*.

Indeed, the more immersed we are in a topic, the more knowledgeable we become, and the more we can lose touch with the audience in question. "Curse of Knowledge" is the notion that once we know something, it is nearly impossible for us to imagine what it is

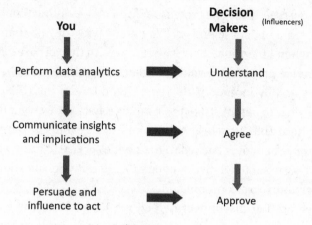

Figure 4-1

like to not know it—in other words, it becomes much more challenging to put ourselves in our audience's shoes, or seats.

To combat these tricky obstacles, I've developed a new leadership communication model, as shown in Figure 4-1.

As the model suggests, effective communication around data involves reaching six key milestones for ourselves (as presenters) and our audiences:

1. **We perform data analytics.** This is often the most time-consuming stage. So all-consuming, in fact, to those in charge of recommending actions and decisions to their superiors that they forget there are five other steps involved! And these five other steps (below) all have to do with telling good stories.

2. **They need to understand the analytics.** Nowadays, many professionals with highly specialized knowledge have to communicate with non-technical counterparts. For example, an insurance actuary must explain to her firm's customer representatives, underwriters, and management how she reached pricing recommendations for premiums for various products. An oncologist consults with patients and fellow medical professionals on the costs and benefits of various treatment options. Often, non-technical audiences

do not understand analytics-related details, but they will not speak up or ask for clarification, whether due to indifference or embarrassment. No matter the reason, a whole lot of time and effort is wasted when your audiences do not understand what you are trying to say at even a basic level. In such circumstances they will not see your value either, so the goal is to ensure basic understanding as a foundation.

3. **We communicate insights and implications.** To be sure, data analytics can be mighty interesting. Don't forget, however, that analytics are a mere means to an end. (Sorry, data scientists!) The ultimate goal of performing data analytics in most settings is for leadership to gain new key insights to make the best-informed decision with available resources. As such, your ultimate goal is to extrapolate these insights and make them abundantly clear early in your communication.

4. **They (hopefully) agree with us.** Even when your audience understands your analytics completely, they may or may not agree with your insights. Have you ever worked with someone who reviewed the same set of data as you but came up with a completely opposite conclusion to yours? Interestingly, when the insights you generate happen to contradict your audiences' beliefs, something powerful immediately and quietly bolsters their entrenched beliefs. Once inertia is embedded within us, it can be impossible to break. And yet where there is a will, there is a way. I will show you how!

5. **We persuade and influence them to act.** Data projects investigate two main sets of questions:

   a. What is happening, or what has happened?

   b. Is what is happening good for us? If so, how can we be sure to capitalize fully on it? If not, what should be done to protect ourselves?

   Persuading audiences in the context of these two questions is challenging. Inertia abounds. Change is hard, so habits are exceedingly hard to break. Once organizational dogma is established, it generates norms, creates beliefs, and guides behavior. So recommending action that goes against norms and beliefs becomes especially challenging. How can you effect change under this circumstance? That's what this whole chapter is about, and in the next sections I'll provide practical tips.

6. **They approve our proposed action.** Leadership is about facilitating positive change in both the short and long terms. To do so, we need others to take action. Everyone loves listening to a story. But what happens afterwards? The best leadership stories facilitate, guide, and prompt actions. Let's talk about how to create such stories.

This model offers a framework for the process and ideal outcomes of data-based presentations. However, now that we know what we want to do, the next step is understanding how we can do it. The first step is to know your audience. As shown in the next section, if you know your audience, you can communicate the data in a way that they can understand the information.

The ultimate goal of your presentation, of course, is action, not just talk. For this reason, once you know your audience, you will want to use the elements and techniques of storytelling to communicate insights and implications, and also to persuade and influence action. In the final section of this chapter, I will cover how to weave data and story into a compelling and inspiring presentation.

KNOW YOUR AUDIENCE: THE FIVE CATEGORIES

Poor understanding of audience composition and needs is why so many data-rich presentations fail to offer satisfying answers, insights, or takeaways. As noted above, there's often a mismatch between what presenters deem share-worthy and what the audience wants to hear. Kimberly Silk, a data librarian at the University of Toronto, emphasizes this point: "The challenge when using data to support evidence-based decision-making is that, while we collect lots of data, and we have lots of answers, we are often guilty of not answering the question [that matters most to the audience]."[5] Going back to my earlier story, if you put yourself in the contractor's shoes, it's easy to see why she thought that the more I know about her efforts on the projects, the more competent she may appear. But from clients' point of view, the more quickly they are given answers they need, the faster they can get on with life and the more value-added their contractors become.

What to do, then?

The answer goes back to the audience: Understanding your audience is *critical* to successful communication. In settings with large volumes of data that can be communicated, knowing your audience is especially imperative. According to a *Harvard Business Review* article, there are five categories into which an audience may fall:[6]

Intelligent Outsiders

These are people who have no previous exposure to your area of expertise or in-depth training in data analytics. They are, nonetheless, intelligent, and oftentimes are well-educated and demanding audience members who are both familiar with your industry and do not appreciate material being dumbed down. For example, financial advisers sit through new product presentations by asset management firms. While they have gone through extensive training and passed rigorous licensing exams, they do not manage assets, are not portfolio managers, and may not understand the complex valuation models asset-management firms use to curate investment products.

High-level Cross-functional Colleagues

These are your organization's "A-Team," colleagues from marketing, operation, finance, accounting, sales, human resources, and other areas, who are familiar with your topic and seek more refined understanding and especially knowledge about how your topic could impact their areas.

The Boss

As in, your boss. This is your direct manager, the person who not only has to understand but also stand by your work. This is the person who will forward your recommendations to higher-ups as if those recommendations had originated from her. In short, the boss may well be taking a chance on her career based on your work. Therefore, she would like to have "in-depth, actionable understanding of intricacies and interrelationships with access to detail."[7]

The Head Cheese(s)

Your manager's managers, or people sitting even higher up in your organization. These are extremely busy executives with little time or patience. They prefer, and often require, conciseness. Many presenters don't appreciate the number of important decisions the Head Cheese must make on a daily basis, and thus might be surprised to realize high-level executives may not know or remember why someone is presenting on a given topic in the first place.

Fellow Experts

Especially in academia, think tanks, or research organizations, it is possible that those in the audience seats are fellow experts who know just as much about your topic as you do, if not more. In this case, explanation, especially in the form of storytelling, takes a back seat. Instead, this audience may prefer to explore and even critique your methodologies and results.

Here, we are assuming that regardless of the audience type, you, the readers, are the data experts. You might not call yourself data scientists. Your role, nonetheless, involves collecting, manipulating, analyzing, interpreting, and presenting data so that you can help your audiences make the most informed and intelligent decisions accordingly.

Understanding which audience type you're dealing with—based on the categories above—is the first step to improving data-rich communications. The Head Cheese will need a very different presentation than Intelligent Outsiders will. Once you have a better handle on your audience's composition and needs, you can move to using "data storytelling" to deliver your message.

WHAT DATA STORYTELLING DOES THAT DATA ALONE CAN'T

You've performed the data analytics and you know your audience, making you aware of what kind of information and data they can process. The next step in the leadership communication model is to share the insights and implications of your data and lead the audience to action. This is where data storytelling makes all the difference.

Data storytelling helps you keep your audience and purpose in mind to communicate data in a way that will address the audience's deepest cognitive needs. Data storytelling is "a structured approach for communicating data insights more effectively to an audience using narrative elements and data visualizations," says Brent Dykes, former senior evangelist of Data Science & Analytics at the software company Adobe.[8] And those narrative elements are not just "extras," fancy flourishes that make your presentation slicker. No, the narrative components are crucial for data-driven presentations because the human mind is built to process stories, rather than cold, hard facts or logic alone. In fact, understanding logic outside the context of a story is much more difficult than processing the same ideas delivered in story form, according to a recent *Scientific American* article.[9]

Story's power comes in part from its engagement of emotion. "Any story we tell of our species, any science of human nature, that leaves out much of what and how we feel is false," notes the *Scientific American* article mentioned above. That's right: not only is a presentation built around human stories more user-friendly for our brains, it also stands a much greater chance of being perceived as the truth. After all, the underlying truth about data is not the numbers themselves, but what the figures represent and mean. "Data scientists want to believe that data has all the answers," Jeff Bladt and Bob

Filbin note in a *Harvard Business Review* article. "But the most important part of our job is qualitative: asking questions, creating directives from our data, and telling its story." Amen.

In the following section, I'll offer a five-step process for effectively telling data's story.

LET THE TELLING BEGIN—A FIVE-STEP PROCESS TO WEAVE DATA AND STORY

Becoming an effective data storyteller requires mastering the following steps and skill sets.

1. **Practice Empathy**: Put yourself in the audience's shoes.
2. **Prove and Persuade**: Know when to do which.
3. **Words Over Numbers:** Emphasize words to ensure retention of key numbers.
4. **Create Meaning**: Identify and emphasize the "so what."
5. **Give Them What They Want, Tell Them What They Need**: Focus on what your audience needs to hear.

STEP 1:
Practice Empathy

In chapter 3, I talked about point of view and how important it was to put yourself in the shoes of your audience. This is especially important for data-based presentations when it is easy to be struck by the Curse of Knowledge: once we know something, it is nearly impossible for us to imagine what it is like *not* to know—that is, to put ourselves in our audience's shoes. Therefore, before you open up PowerPoint and load in everything you think your audience needs to hear, do yourself and everyone else the biggest favor by answering three presentation-prep questions.

Three Prep Questions. Spend time answering these three questions—on your own and with your team—to save a lot of time and energy down the road. You always have the option to go back and refine answers to these questions as you sharpen your message and understand your audience's needs better.

1. What is the makeup of my audience? What do they need to know? (Use the five major categories of audiences presented earlier.)

2. After listening to my presentation, I hope my audience will remember the following points, even if they cannot recall anything else I tell them:

   a. _____

   b. _____

   c. _____

      (up to three major points expressed in 10 or fewer words each)

3. Outside of the project I am communicating about with them, what are the most pressing challenges my audiences face currently? What keeps them up at night?

The answers to these three questions will serve as your guide posts and inform the structure and content of your communication. Additionally, the answers can serve as filters to help you exclude extraneous data and sharpen your presentation.

For example, several years ago I worked with a young client who was a competitive business-intelligence analyst at an online travel company. He had spent weeks researching and then preparing for a business-development presentation. His task was to answer the question of whether his company should expand into a particular foreign market. After going through three drafts of the PowerPoint presentation, he was still staring at close to fifty pages of slides packed with data. Because he had spent so much time and energy on the project, he felt like he could no longer tell what was and what wasn't relevant. So I asked him to go through the Three Prep Questions. Here is a paraphrased version of his responses.

1. **My primary audience** is the senior manager of our strategy team. After listening to my presentation, he will make further recommendations to the CEO of the parent company. He will probably ask a few other people in the strategy group to listen in. But *the Boss* is the key audience.

2. **If my senior manager doesn't remember anything else** from my presentation, I sure hope he will remember that:

   a. No matter what market and product, ease of use (website) is key. [12 words. My client was two words over. Given he only had two must-remembers, I cut him some slack.]

   b. Should expand into the target market immediately. [7 words.]

3. **What keeps this guy up at night?** He is still relatively new to the company. I heard an unconfirmed rumor that he didn't leave his last job voluntarily, and that he was really fired. Why else would he take a step back in his career to take this job? Not just for the love of online commerce! So, he is still trying to prove himself. He will probably grill me on how I come up with my recommendations. Come to think of it, my presentation doesn't only need to be 110% backed by data, but I also need to think of ways to frame the whole thing so it'll make him look like a thought leader, so that he can help us gain a significant advantage over our competitors.

In the process of answering these three questions, my client formulated a mental filter and began to look at his fifty slides differently. Instead of seeing everything as important, he became highly selective of only the information that would help him advance his points. He still had all his data and modeling ready to share, but they no longer were part of the main presentation. Eventually, he cut the presentation from nearly fifty slides down to seventeen.

STEP 2:
Prove and Persuade

Throughout our formal education, we were trained to back up our answers. "Show your work," math teachers reminded us at every school level. Indeed, if we failed to show the steps we had taken to arrive at the answers, we would only get partial credit on exams, if any at all, even for correct answers. So we are conditioned to "prove" our answers and ideas.

The challenge is that the rules of the professional arena are different from expectations in an academic environment. Many of us fail to realize that, in part because no one has informed us explicitly that effective communication in a data-rich environment requires understanding the distinction between proving and persuading.

What's the difference between proving and persuading? *Proving* is mustering the strongest analytical processes and evidence to support your conclusion. *Persuading*, in contrast, is getting your target audience to agree with your point of view and to take action accordingly. Typical scientific research journals such as *Nature* or the *New England Journal of Medicine* are good examples of proving. In such publications, you will read articles that offer research literature reviews, hypotheses, statistical formulas, method write-ups, results, and conclusions written in very technical terms. To gain broad acceptance for their ideas, scientists and other researchers must *prove* the rigor of their findings, question their own studies' limitations, and invite further research to substantiate their conclusions. In a stump speech, on the other hand, a politician *persuades* and rallies voters through carefully crafted communication that uses strategic messages and selective facts to arouse emotion and support.

When crafting stories in data-heavy environments, you need to have content of both types: proving and persuading. So you have to understand the distinction between the two types, as discussed above, and know when to use each. Based on their academic training, most professionals are well prepared to prove points and conclusions. A powerful complement, then, would be adding persuasive content that emphasizes words over numbers and a bias for communicating the "so what." The next two steps will show you how.

STEP 3:
Words Over Numbers

The title implies that words are more important than numbers and therefore should be given preference over numbers. In reality, this approach highlights the critical nature of numbers. How?

Our memory capacity, no matter how large, has its limits. That truth applies to the quantity of numbers we can hold in our brains. In the mid-1950s, psychologist George Miller, who published the paper "The Magical Number Seven, Plus or Minus Two,"[10] established what became the widely accepted notion that an average person can only hold 7±2 numbers in her working memory. Because the space to store numbers is finite, we have to be very judicious about how many numbers we show our audiences.

Table 9. Descriptive statistics and variable intercorrelations in Study 5a.

	1	2	3	4	5	6	7	8	9	10	11	12	13
1. Meta- Dehumanization	-												
2. Meta-Prejudice	.38**	-											
3. Dehumanization	.26***	.04	-										
4. Prejudice	.33***	.38***	.33***	-									
5. Drone support	.10	.07	.27***	.25***	-								
6. Militaristic Counter-Terrorism	.24***	.15**	.39***	.31***	.69***	-							
7. Opposition to Muslim Immigration	.11*	-.03	.31***	.14**	.40***	.39***	-						
8. Signing Anti-ISIS Petitions	.22***	.09	.24***	.19***	.46***	.55***	.27***	-					
9. Anti-Islamic Extremism Fund Disbursement	.11*	.03	.29***	.19***	.54***	.61***	.46***	.42***	-				
10. Encouragement of US soldiers fighting ISIS	.11*	.08	.12*	.01	.23***	.23***	.11*	.24***	.24***	-			
11. Supportive messages to families of Hebdo victims	.07	.12*	.05	.14*	.01	.02	-.06	.14*	.04	.40***	-		
12. Punitiveness towards Hebdo attackers	.29***	.14*	.39***	.33***	.52***	.73***	.26***	.46***	.43***	.23***	.12	-	

Figure 4-2

Luckily, words come to the rescue. Take a look at this example, as shown in Figure 4-2.

This is a table of descriptive statistics resulting from one of ten studies that researchers Nour Kteily, Gordon Hudson, and Emile Bruneau[11] conducted on the effect of inter-group perceptions. In particular, the researchers were especially interested in measuring how "feeling dehumanized by another group can lead you to dehumanize that group in return, which can increase support for aggressive actions against them. Meaning, if Americans think that Muslims see them as savages, Americans will be more likely to return the 'favor,' perceiving Muslims to be savages," as described in an article about the research.[12] Contrast how the author of the article quoted described the key point of the research, versus how the researchers did in their own article, as shown in this excerpt:

> We first assessed whether our manipulation had successfully influenced participants' perception of the extent to which Arabs dehumanized Americans. Indeed, those participants who saw the survey results suggesting that Arabs dehumanize Americans were significantly more likely to report that they were dehumanized by Arabs (M = 4.05, SD = 1.65) than were those who reported that Arabs perceived both Arabs and Americans as highly (and equally) evolved (M = 2.36, SD = 1.29), F(1,153) = 49.20, P < .001, partial η2 = .24. There was also a significant but smaller effect of the meta-dehumanization manipulation on participants' sense that they were disliked by Arabs (high meta-dehumanization condition: meta-prejudice M = 4.88, SD = 1.24; low meta-dehumanization condition: meta-prejudice M = 4.29, SD = 1.32), F(1,153) = 8.18, P = .005, partial η2 = .05.

Of course, by now I hope you've realized that the researchers have to prove their findings, whereas the author of the article only had to persuade her readers about the research's main points. The context is completely different. But the author of the article also had to work to use as few words as possible to describe the key point: whether something is more or less likely to happen. To her readers, the hard statistical facts are less important. Keep in mind, then, that when you can distill the essence of each key concept with words—and ideally not too many of them—you are saving working memory in your audiences' brains for the small set of numbers that truly matter.

STEP 4:
Create Meaning

"Data doesn't create meaning. We do," says Susan Etlinger, an industry analyst with Altimeter Group, where she focuses on data and analytics.[13] In front of her TED Talk audience in 2014, she made the keen observation that in the era of Big Data, we are actually more in danger of making the wrong data-based decisions. Indeed, with access to Big Data comes the temptation to act on what we think we know. As such, data storytellers' job is not just to make sure their audience understands and agrees with their analysis. They must also aim their analysis toward generating implications for decision-making.

Importantly, the data storyteller and decision-maker are often not the same person. In many cases, the ultimate decision-maker sits at a higher level in the organization, and spends part of their precious time listening to presenters like you, seeking analysis and insights as a foundation for their decisions. So, when you facilitate this process well, you are also creating meaning for them. How do you create meaning?

Simon Sinek, author of the book *Start With Why*, offers a simple but powerful answer.[14] In general, nearly everything we present these days can be divided into three categories: Why, How, and What. For example, everyone knows *what* his or her job is. Many know how to do the job. But very few people know *why* they do what they do. Ironically, it is the why that motivates. To create meaning for decision-makers, focus on the whys and the whats of the material you are presenting. And if decision-makers are skeptical of your findings or curious to know more, they will ask how you arrived at your findings.

Taking all of this into account, to structure your communication most effectively, whether a thirty-minute formal board room presen-

Data Story Structure

	STORY	DATA STORY
Beginning	Act 1 Scene Setting	Answers With a Hook
Middle	Act 2 Journey	Context Remind, Recount, and Rename
End	Act 3 Resolution	Action Short and Long Term

Figure 4-3

tation or a five-minute impromptu update for your manager, you can use the Three-Act Formula, one of the Principal Elements of Storytelling described in Chapter 1 (see Figure 4-3).

In Act I, set the scene by diving directly into the answers your audience most likely wants: why they should care and what they should do about it. When you establish Act I effectively, you will also have established a hook. How? Well, exactly. *How?* Once audiences have their questions answered, their natural next questions would be about how you arrived at your conclusions. Perhaps your manager does not quite understand the analyses you used to generate the recommended steps. Maybe the board is skeptical of your recommendations. This makes for the perfect transition to Act II.

Because you have done such a good job setting the scene and establishing the hook in Act I, in Act II you have earned the right to present more on the *hows*. But resist the temptation to data-dump in Act II. Instead, the best way to show your audiences the journey you took is through the 3Rs: Remind, Recount, and Reframe. Don't forget that though you might have spent countless hours on the project, others might not have the slightest idea why they are even attending the meeting. The more highly ranked and organizationally remote your audiences are from you, the more likely this is to be the case. Therefore, *remind* them of the context of the project, along with the gist of project progress and intended outcome. Then you can *recount* the process you used to arrive at the reasons they should care and what they should do. But make sure to stay on a high level to convey the logic; save the detailed calculations or modeling for your presentation's appendix. Last but not least, *reframe* a point of view, even if it represents the slightest change. How have your study, research, and analytics allowed them to see things a bit differently, with new insights? For example, perhaps your organization's conventional marketing approach has been about serving all customer segments equally well. After your analytics research, the data is suggesting that your company dedicates 60% of your total marketing budget to high-value customers. After all, if challenge is the nerve center of story, then change is the soul of it. We are hardwired for story because we love witnessing meaningful change.

In Act III, the closing act, tie back to how it all began, why your audiences should care, and what they should do. In this act, elaborate the actions that will be needed in the short and long term. Then be sure to leave time for questions. And be prepared for them.

STEP 5:
Give Them What They Want, Tell Them What They Need

When you are the one studying and analyzing Big Data, you may well be—or at least feel like—the lone person or team who knows what's best for the organization in a given area. So, you may recognize that the questions your superiors will ask may not be as relevant, timely, or strategically important as they think they are. How, then, do you generate the most value from your analytics while managing up? The following is a real case study (without revealing the company or individuals involved) that illustrates how to "Give them what they want, tell them what they need (to hear)."

Terrence is a design researcher with a tech company well known for its mobile communication products. He reports to both the SVP of marketing and SVP of design. One day, he wondered what role the company's customer service area played in retaining current customers. So he launched a qualitative and quantitative study involving over five hundred current customers. Through his analysis, Terrence uncovered serious, politically charged problems related to the firm's customer-support operations. Just as he was creating his presentation—with those issues front and center—one of his SVPs stopped by his desk.

To Terrence's surprise, the manager told him that the C-suite executives who would be attending his presentation were not really interested in the customer-service experience. Instead, they wanted to know how well the hardware and software were working together for the Sprocket 5000, the firm's soon-to-be-launched high-stakes product. Of course, Terrence had become aware through his study that the company was facing a problem much larger than the performance quality of the new product's hardware and software. But rather than dismissing what his audience saw as important, he took a highly strategic approach to the presentation.

Specifically, on the first slide, he gave his top-management audience what they wanted. His presentation began with an executive summary of the most recent changes in the product hardware and how customers had reacted to them. The summary also included research results of the user experience related directly to the software overhaul. Knowing his executives were particularly interested in the Net Promoter Score (a marketing tool that enables a business to gauge its customers' level of loyalty, which is correlated with revenue growth), Terrence made sure that the NPS results were distilled clearly in the executive summary. But then, the strategic part: He ended the executive summary with a very troublesome number regarding the customer-service experience: there was a 37% decrease in NPS of customers who interacted with customer service, even though the same set of customers did not provide a lower rating for the product itself. Instead of diving directly into the numbers, he told the story of Barbara, a loyal Sprocket customer since the original product's launch who routinely upgraded her devices as soon as they became available. However, Barbara provided a rating of 3 (an extremely low score) on the Net Promoter Score question. Terrence then described Barbara's unsatisfactory experience with customer service.

He then finished the presentation with overall NPS numbers showing that customers who contacted customer service provided a much lower NPS score than customers who had not contacted customer service. In short, customer service was alienating loyal customers.

Terrence's presentation was meant for his two direct managers and several other SVPs. Because of his findings and—more importantly—the way he told the story, his audience truly understood the urgency of the customer-service issue. Consequently, his presentation was escalated all the way up to the CEO and then continued to the parent company, which oversaw customer-support operations and could take action in this area.

Terrence's presentation exemplifies how data storytelling can be effective if done right. Here's what Terrence did right:

1. He told the audience what it wanted to know first, and then what it needed to know.
2. He didn't dive right into the numbers, but rather told a story first (Barbara's story), and then used numbers to emphasize the message of the story: customer loyalty was at risk because of customer service.
3. Throughout the presentation, he balanced clarity and curiosity—one of the most effective ways to tell a story.

Let's talk about the third point a little more. A good storyteller knows how to balance the provision of *clarity*, or giving his audience exactly what they want, and the arousal of curiosity, or prompting them to wonder about important areas that they may not realize are important. But you may ask "Why not aim for 100% clarity in the presentation? Isn't clarity a good thing?" The reality is that two things happen when audiences have complete clarity for any given story. Either they stop listening because they think they have already heard everything they need to hear and they can go back to their phones or laptops or daydreams, or they turn on their inner critic, finding faults and flaws with the presentation. Unless you want to lose their attention or play constant defense, it's best to pique their curiosity by providing inter-

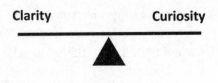

Clarity   Curiosity

Figure 4-4

esting but intentionally incomplete information. The strategic sequencing of clarity and curiosity, as seen in Figure 4-4, will simultaneously satisfy their need to know the basics while encouraging them to want to know more. And that is exactly what Terrence did.

HOW TO TURN 97 PAGES OF DATA INTO COMPELLING STORIES

The specific kind of data story you should tell depends on the research you've done and/or what your audience needs to know. But it remains helpful to think about data and story on a more conceptual and general level. In this regard, Brent Dykes, former senior evangelist of Data Science & Analytics at Adobe, offers the following process.[15] First, he advises structuring a data story around one central idea, emphasizing that "it should have an intended end point or destination that drives discussion and action." Second, he urges analysts to add sufficient relevant context and commentary so that the audience can grasp what the data means. Third, arranging well-explained data in a linear sequence will keep the audience from getting bogged down in the numbers. Finally, as you consider the linear "plot" of your data, consider what else you can borrow from classic storytelling. "Setting, characters . . . and conflict help to engage the audience more deeply on an emotional level," says Dykes.

Let's consider an example that illustrates those ideas.

In August 2015, the US Department of Transportation published a 97-page survey report addressing parking-shortage problems faced by drivers of commercial vehicles on the US National Highway System.[16] Having an adequate supply of parking and rest facilities throughout the highway system is not just a matter of convenience, but also of public safety. The report is exhaustive in its coverage and comprehensive in its reporting. But one can spend hours poring over its hundreds of facts and figures and still fail to grasp the big picture of the problem and its implications. In other words, there are plenty of data elements, but they don't cohere into a central message and set of takeaways. In short, there's a painfully absent *so what*. Below, I present examples from two different articles in which journalists use the story elements of setting, character, and conflict to help a broad audience connect with the report's key issues and insights.

Setting. "The North Bend City Council is considering a ban on more parking for big trucks just off I-90 because of concerns about traffic, exhaust fumes, and the wear on city streets," wrote staff reporter Lynn Thompson of the *Seattle Times*.[17] "But truckers note there is no other full commercial parking area for them between Ellensburg [about a hundred miles east of Seattle on I-90] and Seattle." She continued: "About 900 trucks use Exit 34 daily, according to the city. When Snoqualmie Pass [between Ellensburg and Seattle] closes here because of avalanche control or road conditions, another 300 to 400 stranded trucks park along the freeway." This helps paint a richer picture of the context for the problem, including traffic, road, and weather conditions. Readers can place themselves in the setting easily.

Character #1. "Tracy Giffin, who drives a 75-foot semi out of Idaho, stopped recently between dropping off a load of cargo-handling equipment at Sea-Tac Airport and picking up Genie scissor lifts bound for Montana and Canada." Thompson described what can be assumed to be a typical commercial vehicle driver and their heavy loads, helping readers understand the human side of the issue, including busy drivers' need for parking and rest facilities.

Character #2. The *Seattle Times* reporter also quoted City Administrator Londi Lindell: "What citizens want us to do is preserve the rural character, preserve the natural beauty, preserve the small-town scale. Is it (the expansion of Truck Town) doing those three things? The answer is no." Even in this small excerpt, the voice of a city official wishing to protect her constituents' interests is loud and clear; surely there are many more like her across the national highway system, readers understand.

Conflict. "Where are they supposed to go to the bathroom? Where are they supposed to sleep?" protested Joyce Hibma, a North Bend resident whose husband, Carl, drives long-haul trucks. By inserting a third character, a local resident and a business owner, Thompson further illuminates the intergroup conflict and adds dimension to the parking shortage challenge. "'It's not safe for the drivers to be parked all night along the interstate. Why not give them a place to park?' asked Hibma."

Emotion. Thompson quoted Hibma further to layer in more emotion around the issue: "'Not only are they targeting us and our right to do business, they're targeting truckers as individuals,' she said. 'They have a right to a meal and a safe place to pull into and park.'" Readers can feel the speaker's anger and indignation as she perceives threats to the basic needs and rights of her family and the broader trucker population.

Resolution. Another journalist, Aarian Marshall from *Wired*, presented a state-of-the-art, data-driven solution to the highway problem in her online article.[18] Specifically, a system based on image-processing software can capture parking availability at truck stops and communicate the information to highway signs so that truckers can be alerted early and plan ahead. Scientists are working on this solution already, backed by federal funding. "Papanikolopoulos can't say how many people use the system, but truckers aren't the only ones interested in this information," Marshall quoted the project leader, Nicolas Papanikolopoulos. She continued, ". . . those who run truck stops, perhaps?—to mine the data to help inform business decisions."

These two stories are both about a major problem facing the transportation industry: lack of parking spaces and rest areas for big-rig truckers. The first one provides much-needed story elements: characterization, setting, and conflict among multiple public and private players, including the clash of interests among truckers and town residents/officials. The second article shows how this is a national problem and highlights a promising, technology-based solution. So the articles illustrate perfectly the power of story elements to illuminate data-based insights, implications, and solutions.

If your usual M.O. is to take your audience on a tour of the data with no end in sight—and let's face it, that's what most of us do when presenting data-rich material—it's time to brush up on your storytelling skills. Knowing the story your data is telling, and being able to tell it well, will make your job and your managers' infinitely easier while enhancing results and providing all levels of the organization a compelling narrative to use. This way, everyone can step into the story and act on what they now know—so that in the next story you tell, you all will become the characters who created lasting positive change.

Sometimes data is not the problem; a story can get even more lost in incomprehensible jargon or complicated processes. Using the financial industry as an example, the next chapter reveals the techniques and tools that can make the complexity clear.

CHAPTER 5

MAKING THE COMPLEX CLEAR

*P*ICTURE THIS: YOUR FIRM has been selected as a finalist to be an asset manager for a US multi-employer pension fund, a deal potentially worth millions. Ecstatic, you put together your PowerPoint presentation for the final pitch, then refine it and rehearse it, and refine it and rehearse it again. You want to make it as strong as possible because you know you're up against two other finalists, both more than a hundred times your firm's size!

In fact, one of the other two finalists has been the pension fund's incumbent manager for over a decade, but you're not sure how happy the client is with them, or whether the client is just going through the motions of interviewing other asset managers and will stick with their established partner. Along with all this, you have to keep your audience in mind: the pension fund's board—75 members, 15 third-party affiliates, fewer than 10% of them professional investors. So it's safe to say that most won't understand financial jargon such as "alpha generation" and "attributions."

In this context, how would you ensure that your presentation is substantive, yet understandable and convincing, to those who are investment outsiders? Moreover, how can you craft your firm's story to outshine the others without making your audience feel like they've made a mistake partnering with the incumbent firm?

This story is based on the real-life experience of an acquaintance. But before I tell you more about what actually happened, I invite you to think about a time when you faced a similar situation—when you had to explain a complex idea to someone who didn't know nearly as much about the topic as you did. Maybe you're well known as a pioneer in Roller Equity, and your communications about taxation and deal structures leave even industry insiders bewildered. Or perhaps you've developed a highly effective analytical tool, but its complexity has prospects running back to the familiar (although less advanced) tools they've used in the past. How would you use the many tools introduced in this book to help you in such efforts?

In this chapter, I will use examples from the finance industry—a notoriously jargon-filled industry driven by often-complex processes and ideas—to demonstrate how to use storytelling elements to deliver your communications more effectively. Specifically, you will learn how to:

- **Divide and Conquer:** Separating the mass of complex information you are conveying into categories that will help the audience feel less overwhelmed by the material.
- **Compare the Unfamiliar to the Familiar:** Analogies and metaphors connect the unfamiliar to a personal experience.
- **Use Story Structure as the Foundation:** The AIA structure can lead a wary audience to buy into (and buy!) the unfamiliar.

In each of the scenarios I'll share here—based on real-life situations—strategic application of story made a material difference in the outcome, with lessons that apply to all areas of finance and beyond.

DIVIDE AND CONQUER

Finance is not known for simplicity, with seemingly endless streams of jargon and highly complex quantitative models and concepts. An industry insider needn't go too deep into what she does to confuse those unfamiliar with the field. She can simply use her title! A friend of mine used to be a major bank's head of "institutional derivative sales." To this day I don't know what that means. While those in finance may be able to speak their own language to one another, at least within their own subspecialty, they need to be able to communicate what they do effectively to a broad range of those outside industry or subsector borders.

How to do that?

For one communication strategy, we turn to Joel Moore, a financial adviser who has worked with nonprofits and impact investors since 2003. Moore says that to cut through the thicket of complex financial products, it's best to think of two major product categories: "Loaners," which includes a broad range of products such as bonds, mezzanine debt, peer-to-peer lending, and asset-backed securities (including the notorious mortgage-backed securities from the Great Recession); and "Owners," which subsumes stocks, venture capital, private equity, and real-estate investments, among others.

Most everyone understands that when you *loan* something out, you will (hopefully) get it back with some gratitude. In financial terms, the "gratitude" takes the form of monetary interest paid on the money you loaned. Similarly, when you *own* something, whether a house, a vintage guitar, or the latest smartphone or other technology gadget, you can reap potential benefits of ownership, such as regular use and economic appreciation. In financial terms, the benefits of owning a financial vehicle such as a stock could be dividends or some other form of return on investment.

With this simple framework, Moore is dividing and conquering the complex world of financial products by simplifying jargon-riddled terms into simple categories everyone can relate to. When non-professional investors understand their position better—loaner, owner, or both—they gain a critical sense of orientation. It's like when you enter your high school or college reunion venue, looking into a crowded event room where no one looks familiar. You may feel lost until you spot some familiar faces and head over to say hello. That early sense of familiarity helps you enjoy the entire event, as you meet other old friends and even chat with classmates you never knew well. In the same way, Moore's categories present investors an anchor or starting point that gives them the confidence to proceed. Try the loaner-or-owner dichotomy where appropriate in your own communications, or think about your own divide-and-conquer strategy.

COMPARE THE UNFAMILIAR TO THE FAMILIAR

This section covers the general idea of comparing the unfamiliar with the familiar. In each subsection, we'll consider a slightly different strategy under this theme.

Uwe Schillhorn was the head of emerging market debt at the Union Bank of Switzerland (UBS) in Chicago. Within the asset class he covered, one of the common approaches to gauge investment opportunities is the calculation of risk scores.[1] But Schillhorn didn't use these in his investment process, and his finance-savvy investment clients often asked him why.

Risk scores are mathematical models or tools (like a credit-rating model) that aggregate the financial variables associated with a potential investment—corporate or sovereign debt, in Schillhorn's case—into a single quantitative indicator. Into the risk score go macroeconomic variables of *all* the countries that fit into that specific investment category, including government debt, GDP, external debt, exports, growth, inflation, and others. Once an aggregated risk score across countries is calculated, it can be applied and compared to the overall pricing of the debt-investment opportunities. Pricing and risk generally go together over long periods of time—the lower the risk, the greater the price—but large discrepancies lead to investment opportunities.

But Schillhorn's team didn't use these aggregated risk scores, and when questioned about it, including prospective clients pointing out that competitors used such scores, Schillhorn did not criticize the practice outright. Instead, he shared a comparison related to young people's health levels. Young people as a group tend to have a high "aggregate health score" based on typical fitness indicators such as blood pressure and cholesterol levels, as these tend to be lower on average than those of their older counterparts. But that doesn't mean the health score of a given young individual will always be high.

Take my friend Mike, for example. A current college athlete, he trains rigorously and eats carefully. Not surprisingly, the results of his checkups always came out great. But there's just one problem: Mike had stage-one cancer, and none of the typical checkup exams detected the illness. Luckily, it was caught in time and is treatable.

Schillhorn points out that aggregated risk scores are similar. While the overall risk score of emerging markets as a large *class* of countries effectively represents the economic health of that group, using the average score to represent an *individual* country could be highly misleading, given the complexity of a given nation's risk picture. Consider Venezuela. Its overall economic statistics such as GDP and inflation rate looked strong in the early years of this millennium. But as soon as oil prices declined, all other economic indicators fell dramatically, in part because they'd already been distorted under President Hugo Chavez. Venezuela's dependence on oil and its unstable political regime were the hidden "cancer" that went undetected by the aggregate risk indicators, making what seemed like a strong bet a highly risky one for investors. That's why Schillhorn stayed away from aggregated risk scores. His clients found the health analogy understandable and convincing.

Why does pairing the unfamiliar with the familiar work so well? The research of Larry Jacoby and his colleagues has demonstrated what psychologist Daniel Kahneman captures very well about the unfamiliar-to-familiar link: "The experience of familiarity has a simple but powerful quality of 'pastness' that seems to indicate that it is a direct reflection of prior experience."[2] That is, when you "hitch" an unfamiliar idea to one that is more familiar to your audience, you are creating the sense that the unfamiliar idea is already part of their personal experience, rather than some foreign concept. And since we tend to value our own experience more than any other, we're more likely to buy into the new (but seemingly old) idea.

For example, in September 2016, when Apple announced that the new iPhone—the iPhone 7—would have no headphone jack, enabling greater memory and battery life, consumers and industry observers had highly mixed feelings. But a *New York Times* article made a helpful comparison: "Apple's iPhone, just short of 10 years old, has hit puberty. Like adolescents coping with awkward changes to their bodies, the iPhone 7 . . . introduces some uncomfortable transitions."[3] The analogy, whether intended or not, helped the phone-purchasing public become more comfortable with the new product by relating its evolution to the awkward adolescence life-phase that adults know well.

Another way to bond unfamiliar and familiar is through metaphor. The *New Oxford American Dictionary* defines metaphor as "a figure of speech in which a word or phrase is applied to an object or action to which it is not literally applicable." For example, economist and bestselling author Charles Wheelan explained the statistical concept of the Central Limit Theorem non-quantitatively in his book *Naked Statistics:* "The Central Limit Theorem is the Lebron James of statistics—if Lebron were also a supermodel, a Harvard professor and the winner of the Nobel Peace Prize."[4] Wheelan wanted to introduce the power, elegance, agility, and far-reaching impact of the theorem while staying away from academic jargon. Using an NBA superstar and a world-famous award, Wheelan helped readers understand quickly the basic value of an abstract theorem.

Anyone can use metaphor. We use metaphor frequently in everyday life, as *New York Times* columnist David Brooks noted in his article "Poetry of Everyday Life": "When talking about relationships, we often use health metaphors. A friend might be involved in a sick relationship. Another might have a healthy marriage. When talking about argument, we use war metaphors. When talking about time, we often use money metaphors. But when talking about money, we rely on liquid metaphors. We dip into savings, sponge off friends or skim funds off the top."[5]

STRUCTURE IS THE FOUNDATION

As discussed in Chapter 1, most effective stories share similar structures. A strong structure holds up your story, just as a solid foundation supports a house. A story needs to have an intriguing yet informative beginning, an engaging journey as the middle, and a logically and emotionally satisfying end. This is especially true when dealing with the complex or the unfamiliar. In the next example, an entrepreneur uses the AIA—the story structure discussed in chapter 3—to sell an analytical platform that can help companies change the way they make certain decisions.

To refresh your memory, AIA means: *acknowledge* your audience's experience at the outset; in the middle, *inspire* them to improve their current situations with what you have to offer; and motivate them to *aspire* for a different future at the end—with you as part of it.

My colleague Jason Aitken is a management consultant turned serial entrepreneur. One of Jason's ventures is based on an analytic platform that helps large corporations decide with whom to enter into joint ventures. For example, one of his prime target customers, even before the platform was complete, was a Fortune 100 company with partner-based projects ranging up to $5 billion in capital investment. So deciding on partnerships involved very high stakes for this Fortune 100 company. Not surprisingly, the business tended to fall back on established partners, those they knew best. But that strategy hadn't been working of late. In fact, on average, the firm had been losing up to *$2 million per day* when projects ran overtime due to poor joint venture decisions! Because of the complexity of the projects and the disparate ways that joint ventures are run, senior management had felt that delays in projects' completion were inevitable.

So Jason began his pitch to this prospect not by talking about his product, but by acknowledging the JV-related challenge the firm faced. That can be tricky, as you can imagine that a senior leader might feel embarrassed when an outsider brings up such a serious, largely undetected problem—just as the ultra-rich entrepreneurs felt in our previous example. Thus, the acknowledgment always needs to include components of tact and respect. In this case, it might be something to the effect of "It's easy to see how this could happen to any large firm—after all, it makes sense to rely on trusted partnerships, at least as a starting point."

This last phrase, "at least at a starting point," is a key transition to the next and middle part of the story, and the *I* in AIA: *inspire*. Jason went on to assert that trust and relationship are not sufficient to ensure sound JV decisions and profitability. The assertion enabled him to present a solution that could go beyond trust and established relationships in deciding JV partners: his analytical platform. By acknowledging the prospect's challenge and inspiring them to think beyond their usual way of doing business, Aitken has made the potential customer much more interested in the benefits and features of his product, which he would go into next, emphasizing how the platform addresses their partnership challenges.

Last but not least is your close. Not as in "So, when should we have the next meeting?" (although that should be something you discuss). And not as in "Here's the contract and a pen to sign it" (though that's the end goal). By "closing," in this case, I mean providing a different, *aspirational* (the second *A* in AIA) version of the future, one that you help your prospect picture. In this example, it would be a future where JVs don't lose money and actually return substantial profits, with partnership decisions powered by Jason's analytical platform. Imagination is an underutilized muscle for many professionals today, but one with high impact. So end your story by helping them imagine an alternative future, one that you can help them create. The approach worked very well for Jason: the Fortune 100 firm became his first client, even before his company completed the platform!

PULLING IT ALL TOGETHER: A HAPPY ENDING

As we close this chapter, let's return to our opening example: the asset manager going up against two giant competitors—including the longtime incumbent—in a final-pitch presentation. Spoiler alert: the story has a David-and-Goliath ending, as the manager won the mandate from the multi-employer pension fund. How? Before the pitch, the manager studied his audience closely and became well aware of their wide-ranging experience with investments. Although, in their pitch book, his company was obliged to provide all the numbers and technicalities expected in the industry, he made sure that his presentation minimized the use of jargon, linking the strengths of his funds closely to experiences he believed the audience could relate to. Moreover, he divided and conquered his fund's multi-level strategy into categories that would be easy to understand and remember. Last, he spoke to the importance of providing long-term value to a pension, a value that he personally held dearly. Having previously worked for his multi-national family business, he understood the value of taking care of employees' long-term wellbeing, as he saw his former employees not just as workers, but as extended family he felt obligated to care for. In this way, he used a combination of the approaches this chapter describes, showing his offering's value and evoking an emotional response that helped secure new business.

Storytelling, of course, is not a magic bullet that provides a fairy-tale ending to every business interaction. But using the ideas here can help simplify concepts, make helpful comparisons, and persuade your audience through a powerful combination of logic, empathy, and emotion.

And there is still one technique that we haven't discussed in detail. In the next chapter, I will show you how to blend simple visual elements, data, and story strategically to multiply your persuasive power.

CHAPTER 6

COMBINING THE POWER OF STORY AND SIMPLE VISUALS

WE LIVE IN A highly visual world, but some people struggle with the idea of using simple visuals to tell their stories more effectively. Don't worry: you don't need to be the next Picasso or hire an army of professional designers and illustrators to churn out beautiful infographics. Instead, all you need to know is how to draw a dot and a line. If you can, you already have all the tools you need.

Why are visuals so important? Cognitive psychologist Steve Franconeri, Northwestern University professor and director of the school's Visual Cognition Lab, sums up the impact of visual elements nicely: "If you get your visual on the whiteboard, it dominates the meeting." Most of us would agree that any visual presented, especially an effective one, captures our attention very well as audience members.

This chapter will take you through three main sections devoted to using visuals in your stories: First, we'll learn the Six Types of StoryPicture©. Second, I'll show you how to develop your own unique style to simplify and communicate the complex concepts you use to persuade others. Finally, we'll discuss the nuts and bolts of actually communicating with StoryPicture. By hearing about actual cases, you'll understand how the whole system works and be able to amp up your storytelling power with powerful visuals.

VISUALLY SPEAKING

When we first meet, many of my clients can appreciate the effectiveness of visual elements in communicating complex concepts, having been audience members many times themselves. But most of them don't know why visuals have this power. Very simply, although we have five senses (vision, hearing, smell, touch, and taste), visual inputs take up 40% of our brain resources.[1] That's why our visual fields can dominate other sensory inputs. You may hear a dog's bark, but seeing the dog itself will provide much more information to your brain, helping you decide what to do—for example, does the dog look friendly, or worth running from? In fact, so dominating is visual input that it can *influence what you hear*. A big dog's bark may sound louder than it actually is. All of this means that combining visual elements with what your audience hears will make your communications even more powerful.

That's where the concept of a StoryPicture comes in, or a visual framework used to convey your story more effectively. The process of developing and delivering a StoryPicture-based approach can be strategic and even fun. Here are the basics:

- Anchor your argument with a strong visual framework—the StoryPicture
- Prompt your audience to participate by placing themselves and/or their experiences in your framework
- Use their participation to further inform your communication

Before we go into more detail by introducing the six types of StoryPicture, two disclaimers. One, the StoryPicture are deceptively simple visual elements that will help illustrate parts of stories you want to tell, rather than representing the *whole* stories themselves.

The point is not to use your visuals to illustrate every single detail; rather, they are meant to translate complex and oftentimes amorphous concepts into simple pictures your audiences can understand and follow. Second, the six types of StoryPicture will sound incredibly simple in their descriptions here. The difficulty lies in the execution. Therefore, practicing what you learn here is especially important. No time like the present, so as a first practice step I invite you to take a piece of paper and pen or pencil and select a concept important to you on any level. For example, something important to you personally could be work–life balance, while a concept or priority to you professionally may be strong leadership. Once you've identified this concept, explain what it is specifically and why it's important to you—with words and pictures.

It may be tempting to skip this part. But it's important that you take this step before reading about the tools in this chapter. You might even want to practice with a colleague or a friend who has some understanding of the concept important to you. After you've done this simple step, you can use the concept to practice using the tools I'll introduce, and possibly even return to your work here after reading the chapter to see how you can improve it by using what you've learned.

THE SIX TYPES OF STORYPICTURE

Here are the six types of StoryPicture I've found most effective in storytelling.

TYPE 1:
The Virtuous Cycle

A circle denotes **a system**. An ecosystem, for example, is often based on the idea of a cycle, to indicate the configuration and interaction of the critical elements within this ecosystem. This concept applies to the physical, biological, and mental worlds. It can also be applied easily to the business world. To illustrate, I'll describe how I use this concept to explain my system of mastering storytelling with business impact. I call it the "Virtuous Cycle."

"I can't tell stories," many of my clients say early on. "My cousin can. My grandmother can. My best friend can. But I can't." Some reasons they offer are quite insightful: "When people ask me to tell a story, I just blank out." Others sound more like excuses: "I'm a numbers person. But stories? Not so much."

Whatever their fears about storytelling, I emphasize that becoming a good storyteller is not about innate talent or magical transformation: In fact, it's a rather straightforward process anyone can master. "Think about gold mining," I tell them. At this point, I write the word "Mining" on a piece of paper, as in Figure 6-1.

Mining

Figure 6-1

Then I continue: "All of us are sitting on a gold mine, most of us without realizing it. It's called Life. Our experience, our career paths, memories, trials, and triumphs are all mines we can dig through. But you have to know what to look for. And you have to use the right tools. Doing that makes the process much more systematic, less about luck." (Chapter 7 on Story Collecting will also discuss how mining is a critical and learnable skill.)

"Once you mine the gold ores out of your life experience," I continue, "you've still got work to do, because what you've uncovered isn't yet as valuable as it can be." At this point, I add another part to my evolving Virtuous Cycle visual, as in Figure 6-2.

Then I say: "Just like for gold ore, you have to put what you've mined through a refining process. In storytelling, refinement is about using structure, plots, obstacles, and everything else you've learned from previous chapters. In the refining process, you'll separate what's important from what's not. Again just like gold, your end product will 'weigh' less but be much more valuable: a concise, compelling story.

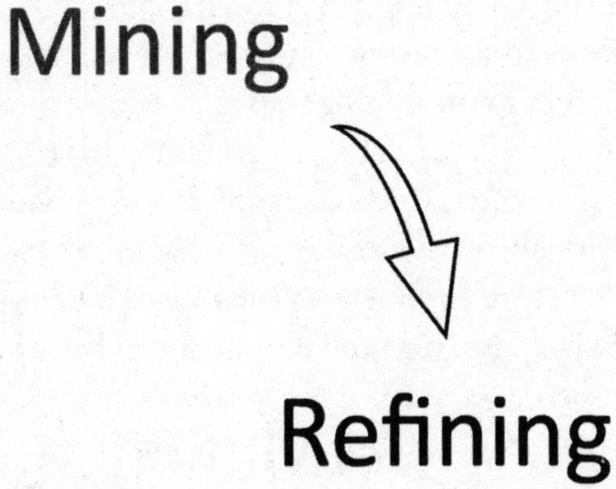

Mining

Refining

Figure 6-2

"But you're not done yet. Just because you have what you think is a refined story doesn't mean that your audience will understand and appreciate it. So the final step in completing the Virtuous Cycle is by figuring out the most effective way to tell the story." Now I complete my picture with one last component: *telling*. Then, I add the word "Telling" and another arrow to complete my visual, as seen in Figure 6-3.

I also point out that how they use the story, once it's fully mined and refined, is up to them, just like gold may end up in jewelry, a

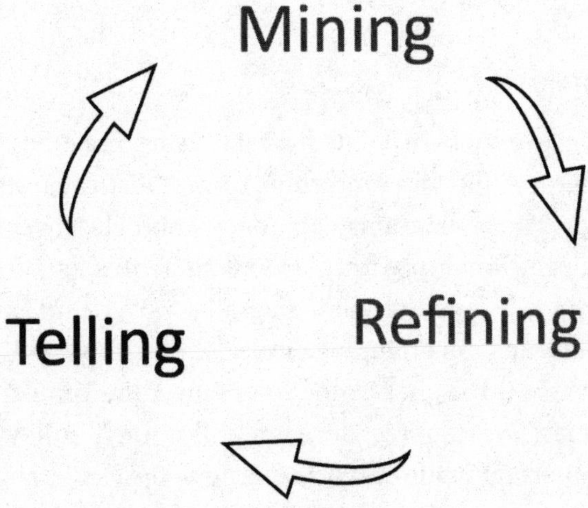

Mining

Telling

Refining

Figure 6-3

trophy, or even a dental filling. "You have to tell your story to your target audience to see how well it works," I tell them, "then refine it further or return to the mining step to develop a new, more effective one. Therefore, there is a sub-system connecting *telling* back to *refining*." Now my Virtuous Cycle is complete, as in Figure 6-4.

The bigger point of this discussion is that you can use the Virtuous Cycle StoryPicture to illustrate how any given system works, by showing the configuration and interaction of key components.

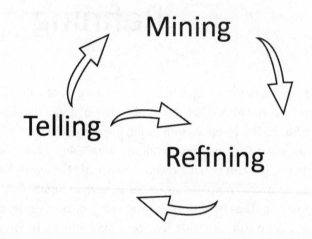

Figure 6-4

TYPE 2:
Venn Diagram

You see them everywhere. Venn diagrams using circle-based graphics appear widely to illustrate everything from statistical probabilities to color charts. These diagrams can quickly and clearly establish the nature of a **relationship** within or among people, qualities/behaviors, and things. While the Venn diagrams most people are familiar with are made up of overlapping circles, the example I will use as an illustration here is the lesser known version of the Venn diagram, the **nested circles**. For example, here is a philosophy I follow regarding anything important in life or work. It is depicted as two circles nested within a larger one, as seen in Figure 6-5, with the word "Norm" in the middle of the smallest circle.

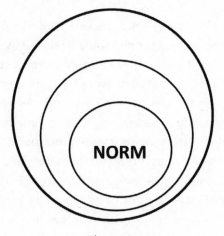

Figure 6-5

When explaining it to others, I say, "Here we have three overlapping circles. In the middle of them is what I consider the norm, in this case a behavioral norm: what's considered 'normal' about what people do, say, wear, represent themselves, interact with others—basically what everyone expects of one another given the specific culture and social context." So, if the center represents the norm, then the edge of the largest circle is where things would be considered, as in Figure 6-6.

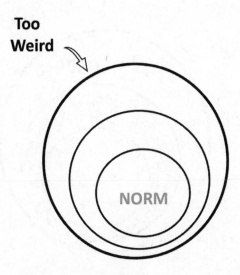

Figure 6-6

By "too weird" in Figure 6-6, I mean overly different or unexpected, so far from the norm that people would likely fail to understand it or, worse, start looking for an exit. For example, a colleague told me about someone she'd met at an alumni event for her college: "The guy announced he was in the car-repo business and specialized in 'creating misery for people who were too greedy,' then chuckled about it while I just stared at him." In this case, it wasn't just the odd sense of humor on display, but the speaker's pride in doing something that caused real pain for a wide range of car owners; while some of them might have been seen as extravagant, most of us can empathize with the many others who lost jobs or suffered other issues that made them unable to make their car payments. My friend said she made an excuse and left the conversation, and noticed how many others did the same thing to the gleeful misery-maker throughout the event. Too weird.

But Norm-ville and Too-Weird-land aren't the only territories on my Venn diagram. In fact, I like to occupy the region indicated by the squiggly line in the StoryPicture, which we can think of as my "just right" space. (See Figure 6-7.)

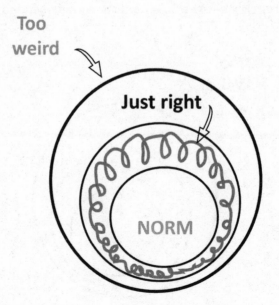

Figure 6–7

I like to be different, but not to the point that people may find it hard to accept me or hear my message. For example, in all my training sessions and workshops, I always play music before the event starts, during breaks, and at the conclusion. My favorite Pandora station for this music is *The Hot Club of San Francisco*, which features tracks marked by the major mode, violin or acoustic guitar solos, and a mid to fast tempo with an obvious swing influence that pumps much-needed energy into what could be an otherwise sterile, bland office space. I also request an event seating arrangement that closely resembles that of a café. Whenever feasible, I steer clear of boardroom- or classroom-style seating. All of this means that when participants walk into my events, they notice that something is different—in a good way—but often can't articulate why.

Notice how the three circles in my StoryPicture aren't perfectly concentric—that is, they don't all have the same center. That's intentional. As you may know from experience, some groups allow very little space for deviation from the norm, as illustrated by the X in Figure 6-8.

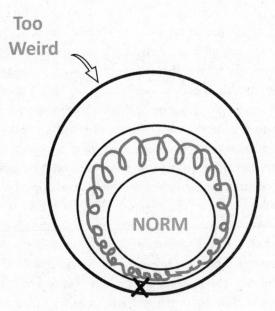

Figure 6–8

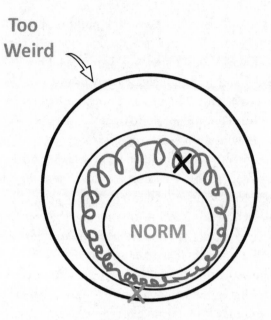

Too
Weird

Figure 6-9

Other groups, in contrast, may allow much more latitude before considering a given behavior too weird, as suggested by the dark X in the middle region below, in the fully completed diagram in Figure 6-9.

As you can see, deviating the same distance from the norm would land me in the realm of too weird for a group with strict norms but might be barely noticeable to a more accommodating group. Understanding this is particularly important for all of us as we prepare to address a given audience. "How different is too different?" we should ask in developing our communications for them.

When I present this StoryPicture, I usually stop at this point to ask my audience to reflect on their own experience. A core power of using a StoryPicture to communicate lies in the opportunity to have your audiences use the framework to share their own stories. In the case of the StoryPicture example here, audience members could add their own "X," thus creating a new image that reflects their experience. In general, when you present your StoryPicture, you are effectively anchoring the audience with your framework for thinking about the world or a particular issue, subtly gaining buy-in from them.

Note that while the circles in my example are nested (which we could call **total overlap**), you can certainly have a Venn diagram with circles that don't overlap at all, indicating two or more elements with no relationship, no interaction, and therefore complete independence from one another. Or you could have a Venn diagram with circles that overlap partially, the more typical image most people hold of such a visual. The size of the overlapping area not only indicates how much these two elements have in common, but also usually reflects a new characteristic. For example, a red circle overlapping a blue circle will yield an area of purple where they intersect. A circle representing the idea of hard work may be overlapped with one symbolizing luck to give us some people's concept of success (when hard work meets luck). The more circles you have, the more additional elements—and potential areas of overlap—you are introducing.

In sum, my Venn diagrams help us anchor our point of view with our audience by establishing visually how we portray relationships within and among people, qualities/behavior, and things.

TYPE #3:
The Graph

Graphs can be used for many purposes. Most depict a **pattern, relationship, process, change, or some combination**. For example, a graph may show the fluctuating prices of oil and stocks over time, or population growth and decline. Similarly, author Kurt Vonnegut described the Shape of a Story by using a graph with one axis representing a character's good or ill fortune and another representing time—a simple but brilliant way to plot story lines as a reminder of chapter 2 in Figure 6-10.

While many people have devoted a lifetime to studying literature and stories, describing their complex structures and components, Vonnegut's minimalist Shape of a Story graph highlights the simple elements at the heart of many stories: fortune, as a function of time. Has he left out other important parts of stories? Of course. There is no mention of emotion, for example. Nor did he include point of view. Still, his graph offers a compelling framework for discussion of most

Boy Meets Girl

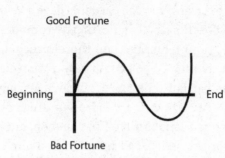

Figure 6-10

books, films, plays, and TV shows, not to mention the rise and fall and rise again of real-life individuals or organizations.

Toward this chapter's end, I'll show you a more extensive example of a graph used for business communication. For now, remember that a graph shows **pattern, relationship, process, change, or some combination**, making it a very versatile StoryPicture.

TYPE 4:
The Pie Chart

Okay, I know the concept of a pie chart is pretty simple. But when used in the right circumstance, this fourth type of StoryPicture can communicate your core message with great power. I heard one of the best examples through the popular *Freakonomics* podcast, when the series explored the possibility of merging the US and Mexico. That's a controversial, provocative question for a number of reasons. Other than the logistical and cultural feasibility of integrating two countries, the topic raises fears of modern colonialism. But the *Freakonomics* franchise has made a name for itself by asking—and trying to answer—unaskable questions. This specific episode featured interviews with economists, politicians, and even the former Mexican president Vicente Fox. The last interviewee was Austan Goolsbee, University of Chicago professor and former chairman of President Obama's Council of Economic Advisers (CEA). Stephen

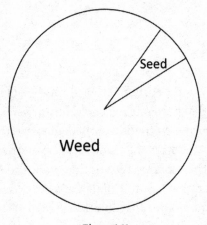

Figure 6-11

Dubner, host of the show, asked "What do you think? Is it [the merger] a good idea?"

"An old friend of mine who was on the CEA many years ago gave me this advice when I took the job," Goolsbee answered. "A good CEA Chair [is] like a good gardener, [whose job] is 90% pulling weeds and 10% planting seeds. So, we're going to see if this is in the weed category or the seed category."[2] See Figure 6-11 for what the pie chart would look like if Goolsbee were to draw one.

Though Goolsbee couldn't draw a picture for the listening audience, he alluded to simple figures that would be easy to visualize with a pie chart like the one above. In effect, he encouraged listeners to judge the question's merit using his weed-or-seed framework. Does the issue of a US–Mexico merger belong to the pulling-weeds category, or does it represent a seed with strong growth potential?

Note that the **weight and proportion** of a pie chart is crucial. It's probably fair to guess that about 90% of Goolsbee's job was indeed about "pulling weeds," or recognizing that a given idea or issue was not worth discussion or might even be potentially harmful to pursue. In the podcast, Goolsbee deftly indicated that Dubner's question was probably not worth much consideration, due to the merger's impracticality and controversial nature, without ever saying so explicitly, allowing the audience to reach this conclusion on its own.

TYPE 5:
The Formula

Have you ever heard of "physics envy"? It's a term that arises from (mostly) friendly competition between physicists and social scientists. In the world of hard science, including physics, researchers follow specific scientific methods to collect data, perform analysis, and generate laws or theories that tend to apply across circumstances. Gravity works the same way whether you are in the center of Manhattan or on top of Mount Kilimanjaro. An even simpler example is that 2 + 2 = 4, no matter the situation. Social scientists, too, apply their own scientific methods and collect data, but many of their findings about basic phenomena tend to be subject to exceptions and to be dependent largely on context. Hence the idea that non–hard-science fields may "envy" physics and similar subjects for their ability to uncover relatively stable, global rules and principles, or what could be thought of as **governing principles**.

A formula, our fifth StoryPicture, is a way of illustrating a governing principle, or a rule that applies to a relationship among several elements. Take a look at the example in Figure 6-12.

The first picture illustrates the *drinking* of an alcoholic beverage; the second is a vehicle's steering wheel, representing *driving*. The last image clearly symbolizes *death*. Drinking + driving = death. Will drinking and then getting behind the wheel of a car or other vehicle always lead to death? No, of course not. But by adopting the "halo of certainty" of hard-science rules through use of a visual formula, the message is made that much clearer: driving under the influence of

Formula

Figure 6-12

alcohol exponentially raises the probability of traffic-related death or injury.

Another example of a formula is the Idea Quotient. Long ago, I worked with someone we'll call Tom (not his real name). Tom was a very capable person: ask him to do anything, and he would deliver. I loved working with Tom. The only thing is, he talked. A lot. He shared a great deal of information, whether useful or relevant to his colleagues or not. If there were a big event coming up and I said "Tom, how can I help you?" he'd launch into a 15-minute monologue, talking twice as fast as I do! On top of that, by the time Tom stopped speaking, most of us weren't sure exactly what his main point was—or if he even had one.

The effectiveness of someone's communication skills can be expressed as the number of ideas they convey divided by the number of words it takes to communicate them. Instead of using twenty-seven words, which is what I just did in the previous sentence, to describe this concept I can use a formula, as seen in Figure 6-13, to express the same thing but much more simply.

In other words, the fewer words used to explain an idea, the more skilled the communicator. While I haven't done specific research on this simple formula—which I made up myself—I think it's hard to argue with. For example, everyone would agree that saying "Stop!" is a more effective way to communicate an idea than "It would be of great value to me if you would desist the activity in which you are currently engaged" (sorry, lawyers!). So think of the Idea Quotient as the $E = mc^2$ of the communication world (sorry, Einstein!). More importantly, think of your own formulas to illustrate ideas you wish to communicate.

Formula

$$\frac{\text{One Idea}}{\text{Number of Words to Explain Idea}}$$

Figure 6-13

TYPE 6:
FEE (Freestyling for Everything Else)

This category covers any other StoryPicture that can be effective but doesn't fall neatly into the previous five categories.

For example, during training sessions or workshops, I sometimes ask my audience to explain the difference between "alumnus," "alumna," "alumnae," and "alumni." At most only one or two people can—it gets tricky, involving dimensions of both gender and plurality. Explaining the answer in words is challenging, to say the least. But a simple chart, in Figure 6-14, can quickly convey the concept (with some accommodation for the clothing-based gender stereotypes!).

As the chart displays elegantly: a lone male former student is an "alumnus"; a lone female former student an "alumna"; a group of all female former students "alumnae," and a group of all male or mixed

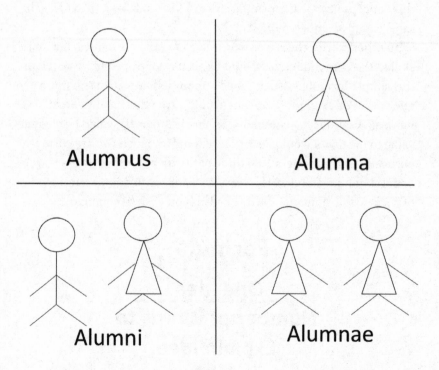

Figure 6-14

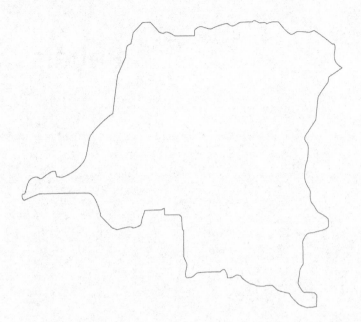

Figure 6-15

former students "alumni." Five groups, four confusing terms, one simple graphic, zero need for a crash lesson in Latin.

Another example of a freestyle StoryPicture involves the intersection of investment and fear. A client of my client often had to explain why their oil investment in the Republic of the Congo wasn't reason for concern, despite the ongoing civil war in a country that shares a very similar name. First he drew a rough outline of the war-torn country that shared a similar name, such as Figure 6-15.

When prospective investors raised questions about the risks related to the ongoing civil war, the executive presenting the opportunity used the map to highlight where the rebels had concentrated their fight: the northeast, as seen in Figure 6-16.

Then he drew a line through about the middle of the country like in Figure 6-17.

The line didn't represent any official border or demarcation. But it helped the presenter make his next point, while adding the most important element to his StoryPicture, in Figure 6-18.

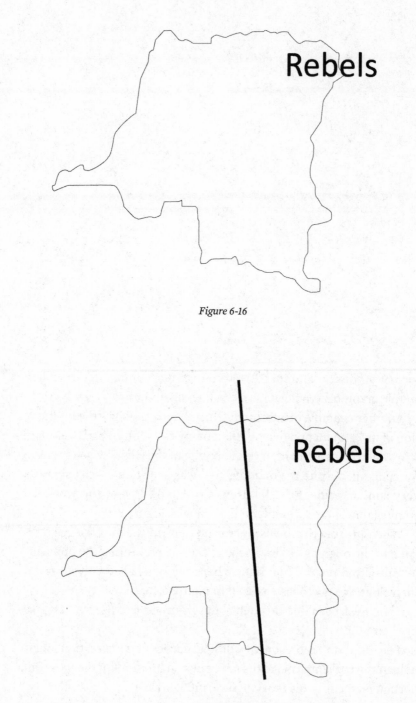

Figure 6-16

Figure 6-17

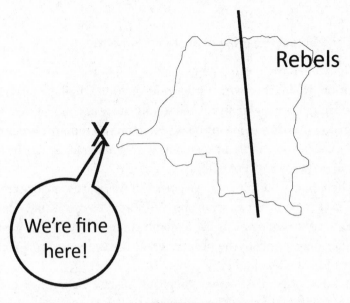

Figure 6-18

This last piece shows the audience exactly where the oil invest-ment is—in a safe area far from rebel activity. In fact, the investment is actually in the Republic of the Congo, a wholly separate country from the strife-ridden Democratic Republic of the Congo, as the pre-senter points out at the end. But just saying that in words isn't nearly as powerful as using the map-based, real-time StoryPicture to drive the message home.

MAKE YOUR OWN STORYPICTURE

Now that you know a lot more about StoryPicture, it's time to practice using them. This section covers how to create your StoryPicture: how to decide which type of visual to use among the ones discussed ear-lier, and how to draw it to best support your story/communication. To illustrate the five steps involved, I'll use a StoryPicture I helped my colleague Shivani develop for her own personal communication challenge.

STEP 1:
List and Select the Most Important Elements

I highly encourage using paper and pencil—or pen, or any writing instrument—for this work, rather than anything digital. Start by listing all important elements related to your story or concept. Just write them down as they come to you, and don't try to refine or order them just yet. Brainstorming the elements with someone else can be helpful, if you (and they) are willing.

Then, once you think you've got a full list, start to prioritize. You may have generated twenty or thirty different elements, but now you need to try to narrow this list to about three to five of the most important ones to make the best progress toward your StoryPicture. Here's Shivani's example.

In 2014, Shivani's brother and sister-in-law visited her and her parents in the Midwest. The young couple lived in San Francisco and was trying to start a family. After a few bumps in the road, they were finally expecting! Her sister-in-law was twenty-eight weeks pregnant, which the couple figured gave them plenty of time for a quick family visit, returning well before the due date.

They were wrong. During their trip, Shivani's sister-in-law had to be rushed to the hospital for an emergency C-section. The baby girl was born and taken immediately to the NICU. "She'll need to be in the hospital for at least three months," the doctors said about the newborn. During this stressful period, Shivani's newly extended family had to focus on how to handle the emotional roller coaster they'd been forced to ride.

In this context, we decided to develop a StoryPicture to help Shivani communicate with her family about the situation, starting with a list of all key elements, as below.

- Goal
- Stuff happens
- Mindset*
- Energy
- Outlook

- Action
- Words
- Control*
- Feelings/emotions
- Hope
- Faith
- Love
- Stress
- Uncertainty
- Focus
- Marginal impact
- Beliefs

Over multiple conversations, we chose those that seemed the most important, going more with intuition and emotion than a more structured process. Shivani decided mindset and control were most important (as noted by the asterisks above), given her family members' personalities and the specifics of their situation. She wanted to help her family members develop a mindset that would make them feel that they had some control over the situation.

STEP 2:
Understand What Binds Key Elements

Once you prioritize the elements successfully, consider the primary *binding agent* associated with the elements you've chosen, or what helps tie them together. Is it about a system, a relationship, or a process? Is it weight and proportion? Governing principle? Or something else that you're trying to illustrate? To refresh your memory, here are the binding agents associated with each type of StoryPicture, as outlined in Table 6-1.

This is the messy—I mean, creative—part. The binding agent determines which StoryPicture will be most effective. But you may find yourself with a bad case of physics envy (discussed earlier) because there's often no one right answer: different binding agents may work for the same set of elements. In Shivani's case, we first settled

Type	Style	Binding Agent
1	Virtuous Cycle	System
2	Venn Diagram	Relationship
3	Graph	Pattern, relationship, process, change
4	Pie Chart	Weight and proportion
5	Formula	Governing principle
6	FEE	Varies

Table 6-1

on using *process and change* as the binding agent because the situation involved a medical process to help the baby grow and develop, the desired change. And it would certainly involve the process of family members supporting one another throughout. So the first StoryPicture we came up with was the graph in Figure 6-19, with the two elements of mindset and control going from negative to positive along their respective axes.

Shivani was satisfied enough with our progress, and we decided to leave it alone for a few days, which is always a good idea, as long as you have the time. But when we returned to the StoryPicture, it no longer spoke to Shivani; she just didn't feel inspired by it the way she wanted to. We knew that meant it was literally back to the drawing board. Don't settle for a StoryPicture that doesn't work for you, as it most likely won't work for your audience either.

As we thought more about it, we believed we should focus the family on the elements of beliefs, mindset, and actions, as part of a *system*, as depicted in the virtuous cycle StoryPicture in Figure 6-20.

Ultimately, we believed that while the original graph would have been best for a communication goal of helping the family reflect or diagnose their situation, it was better to use the virtuous cycle, for two reasons. First, Shivani couldn't think of any story that would go

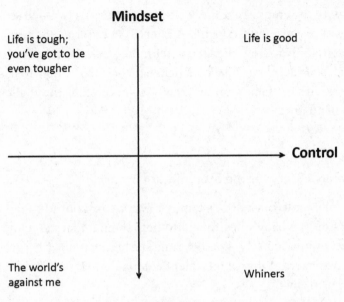

Mindset

Life is tough;
you've got to be
even tougher

Life is good

Control

The world's
against me

Whiners

Figure 6-19

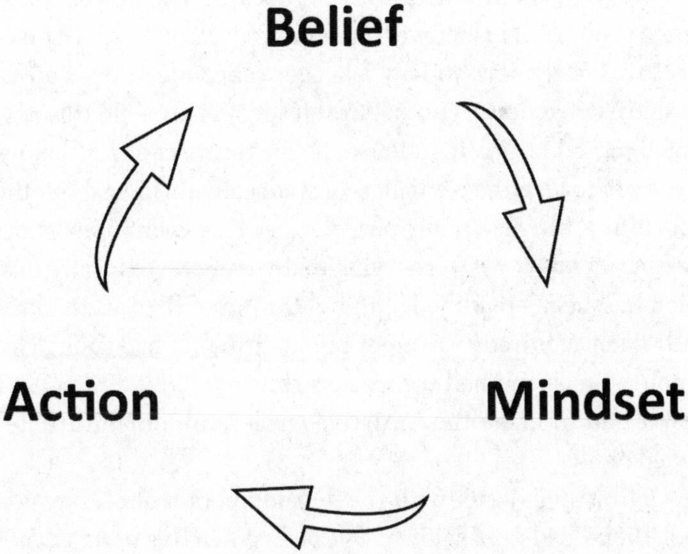

Belief

Action

Mindset

Figure 6-20

well with the graph. Two, the cycle StoryPicture has a much stronger element of cause-and-effect: if A, then B. The stories she wanted to tell her family to help them cope with the stress lent themselves to this idea of causality, and would help her share a roadmap to positive change with her family, rather than just emphasizing the challenging state of affairs.

STEP 3:
Develop a Story for the StoryPicture

Shivani decided to tell her family a work story both to take their minds off the baby's health and to help them understand and deal with the situation. The story was one she had shared with a group of new managers at one of our client companies. Here it is, as told to those managers:

> **Beliefs.** It's not something we commonly talk about in business, but it's something that truly impacts your team and your project. And I had an opportunity to experience this firsthand, in two very opposite situations. The first was when I was working as a product manager with an online community space business. I was fairly new, and my manager called me into his office and said, "Great news: One of our salespeople just sold this new campaign, and I think it's going to be the future of our company. I want you to lead the campaign." I was really thrilled about the opportunity, but also really nervous, because even in my short time there I knew we were trying to diversify revenue streams, which had been steadily declining. On top of that, we had recently been acquired by a larger public firm that had spent a lot of money on us and had yet to see a return on investment. So I knew I had to make the initiative successful; our future depended on it.
>
> As a first step, I met with the development team. They just shook their heads and said, "We've been down this path. It's not going to work." Next, I spoke with my fellow product manager, who said, "I understand. This is a revenue-generating initiative,

so it takes priority over others like user-interface issues." But the project managers of all the other areas were upset, because now they would lose resources for the projects they thought critical for the business.

Last, I spoke to the salesperson who'd sold the high-promise campaign in question. Unfortunately, it sounded like he'd just wanted to sell something shiny and new, without really considering the business's core competencies or even speaking with the rest of us about what was most feasible. Still, I continued to lead the initiative and, and after spending many hours and resources—a lot more than expected—I was able to deliver on this campaign and the client was very happy with the results. But our sales team was unable to replicate the initiative and sell it to any other clients.

Over the two years I was there, we went through four different VPs of sales. Shortly after I left, a new CEO was brought in to cut costs, and he eventually sold the company for pennies on the dollar. So what did I learn? In this case, many people didn't **believe** in the product, and that directly impacted their **mindset**. I got a lot of "Really? Are we really going to do this?" That influenced colleagues' **actions** (including reluctance to give up resources for the new initiative) and ultimately helped lead to the poor outcome for the company.

Luckily, I've also seen the opposite happen. Many years ago, I was brought in as a consultant for a large consumer-goods company to help them with a sales-and-marketing software implementation. When I got there, people were very skeptical. My colleagues didn't **believe** in this project. They had done a software integration before and knew it often took longer than expected, cost more than originally thought, and didn't necessarily deliver expected results. Fortunately, the client VP overseeing the project took a strategic approach: he brought in project champions from within and outside the organization and threw a huge kickoff party at a fun restaurant with music, food, and drink, presenting the inspiring vision for what sales and marketing would look like after the integration.

People were really excited, and on top of that we all felt privileged that we were part of the team that was going to make this change happen. Sure, the project itself wasn't always smooth sailing, but everyone came together to address all challenges with creative solutions. Throughout, we had fun together, pulling pranks on each other and holding a Secret Santa exchange over the holidays. The kickoff had set a great tone for the project, and we truly enjoyed working together. As a result, we delivered even before expected, and we had the highest adoption rates from the sales and marketing team that the company had ever seen.

This just goes to show you that truly **believing** in the product and the cause that you're working on directly impacts the **mindset** of the team, with clear influence on people's **actions** and, eventually, the outcome. So, as a new manager, please take some time to think about what you believe in, what makes you get up in the morning, and how that's going to impact your team and your outcomes.

Those were the stories Shivani planned to tell her brother and sister-in-law to help them adapt to their challenging situation. But how best to tell the stories?

STEP 4:
Try, Test, Gather Feedback

In this stage, you experiment with ways of telling the story, using the StoryPicture and gathering valuable feedback. Shivani tested her StoryPicture with her brother first, because her sister-in-law was understandably experiencing more stress about the baby. Initially, Shivani only planned to tell the positive story. However, her brother reminded her that his wife was a critical thinker who naturally questioned things that sounded too good to be true. So Shivani decided to present both the positive and negative stories to her sister-in-law, to make the message stronger by showing two different situations in which beliefs, mindsets, and actions worked together to influence outcomes.

STEP 5:
Repeat and Refine, Refine and Repeat

Think of this as the polishing stage, where you think hard about final touches to the StoryPicture, the story that accompanies it, and how best to present these. Shivani took about a week to think about it, repeating the story to herself and others before sharing it with her sister-in-law, the baby's mother. Repeat and refine. (In our example, we made multiple refinements to the StoryPicture and accompanying stories before developing the polished ones I shared in the earlier steps.)

As she prepared to share the story with her sister-in-law, she imagined asking her sister-in-law whether she saw parallels between the work situations in the story and the family's stressful healthcare situation. She didn't need to: her sister-in-law's brow furrowed in concentration as Shivani told the stories, and at the end she said "Shivani, I see how what you're saying relates to what we're going through." She understood that what they believed about the baby's health and situation would influence their ongoing mindset and the actions they took, likely influencing the outcome.

For Shivani's brother and sister-in-law, the StoryPicture and story ultimately helped them focus on maintaining positive beliefs as part of a proactive, optimistic mindset that enabled them to take healthy actions (working carefully with doctors without overburdening them, taking time for themselves despite the ongoing stress, and others) that allowed them to navigate a very stressful situation. Their baby girl came home a whole month earlier than the doctors predicted. At the time of this writing, she's a very active, happy, healthy two-year-old!

STORYPICTURE BEST PRACTICES

Here are some of the best practices I've developed for making the most effective StoryPicture.

1. **Always have something to write with and to write on.** The best way to communicate a StoryPicture, perhaps ironically, is to not make a big deal out of it. No pomp and circumstance, no big announcement or unveiling. For example, in a group setting you could casually go to a whiteboard or poster-paper and use a marker (make sure at least one is working ahead of time!) and draw your visual while telling the related story. Or you can do this with pen and paper in a more individual setting. A latent benefit of the StoryPicture is that it allows you to be in charge of the conversation by putting you in the spotlight with your visual as you draw it for the audience.

2. **Tell your StoryPicture in the beginning of a meeting/presentation.** Doing this sets the stage, anchors your audience to your framework, and gives them something to think about and work on. In negotiation, the party who announces their demands anchors the issue in question. In marketing, suggested pricing anchors consumers' sense of product value. Using a StoryPicture acts the same way.

3. **Save your best for never.** Do *not* include your best StoryPicture in any pre-printed materials. If you include your best visual in your pitch book, for example, it will have to compete for attention with everything else in the book. More importantly, when something is being sketched out right in front of your audience members' eyes, it conveys a sense of newness, something fresher than a pre-packaged idea. Whether you just grab a cocktail napkin or go to a whiteboard, you're conveying that you're showing them something that has just occurred to you, even if it actually occurred to you long before. This makes them let their guard down and become more open to what you have to say. Printed materials these days tend to be overly polished and come with many bells and whistles. Ironically, this decreases excitement. However, when you tell a StoryPicture, you are representing your thoughts in a more "primitive" but more

inviting way. It draws people in, and makes them wonder "Where is this going?"

4. **Practice telling and drawing, and the timing between telling and drawing.** Don't be fooled by how easy using a StoryPicture may seem. When you watch a well-told StoryPicture unfold, it will seem impromptu, as the item above suggests. In reality, most people need to figure out ahead of time what part of the visual goes before or after its corresponding piece of the story for maximum effect, just as a magician must practice a trick countless times to get it just right. The more you practice, counterintuitively, the more spontaneous your StoryPicture seems, and the more effective it becomes.

Using a StoryPicture is easily one of the most straightforward, natural, and cost-effective ways to amplify the power of your message. I encourage you to make the most of this story approach.

In the final chapter of this section, I will show you that collecting stories is one of the secrets of becoming a great storyteller.

CHAPTER 7

COLLECTING STORIES FROM EVERYWHERE

*T*HE FIRST TIME I studied storytelling in a formal setting, I was lucky to have professor Rives Colin of Northwestern University's theater department as my guide. It was nearly fifteen years ago, but I still remember one important lesson: finding the right story to tell for a particular audience can easily take up half of one's total preparation time for any important presentation/communication. And guess what? As storytellers, there are only so many stories we can draw on that are based on our own personal experience. Collecting stories, therefore, becomes an ongoing task for any storyteller serious about mastering their craft. Just as teachers, physicians, lawyers, accountants, and many other professionals take continuing education courses to gain new skills and maintain their licenses, so should storytellers self-impose a professional standard of collecting stories regularly.

This chapter shows you how to do that: how to collect stories by first asking crazy good questions that help your audience generate their stories, and then by listening aggressively.

WHY STORY COLLECTING MATTERS

At this point, you still may not be convinced that story collecting is necessary. Beyond the idea mentioned above that you have only a finite number of stories to tell based on personal experience, here are several other reasons story collecting is critical.

Practice

A competitive swimmer needs to start her training early in the morning, six days a week. A professional actor spends hundreds of hours rehearsing, alone and with his troupe, before a performance. Even with an abundance of natural talent, mastery requires hours and hours of dedicated practice—as much as ten thousand hours minimum, by some accounts![1] Then why can't storytellers just tell endless stories? That *is* practice, isn't it? True enough, but telling lots of stories alone will not be sufficient. Mastering storytelling is a process similar to mastering writing. While it's inherently true that writers write, writers also have to read—a lot! Stephen King said in an interview with National Public Radio: "If you want to be a writer, you must do two things above all others: read a lot and write a lot. There's no way around these two things that I'm aware of, no shortcut."[2]

In the same way, storytellers have to hear and collect many stories. This is not only to immerse yourself in the world of great stories, though that is certainly helpful. Nor is it just to know a lot of stories, which also comes in handy. But it is also, critically, about building a bridge with the one thing that matters most in storytelling: your audience. Specifically, collecting stories connects you with your audience's point of view, to understand what matters to them and motivates them; moreover, when you collect stories from your audiences, their stories can ultimately become *your* stories.

Point of View

We covered this topic extensively in chapter 3. In the current chapter, however, I would like to introduce you to veteran storyteller and

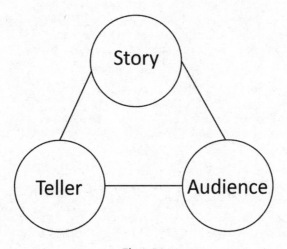

Figure 7-1

teacher Doug Lipman's storytelling model,[3] in which point of view plays the role of bonding you to your audience and your story to your audience, as suggested by the graphic in Figure 7-1.

Most every time someone tells a story, someone else is listening. Thus, there are three elements involved: the story, the storyteller, and the audience. The three lines represent the connections among these factors, and each bond can be strong, moderate, or weak. For example, say you're pitching a new idea to a cross-functional team within your company, but you don't really believe in the idea yourself—you may be presenting it on your manager's behalf, for instance. Here, the idea pitched is the story, you are the teller, and your colleagues are the audience. We'll use Lipman's model to illustrate this example, in Figure 7-2.

Suppose further that your colleagues do not have strong feelings about the idea, positive or negative. So the line connecting the story and the audience is solid, if not especially strong. However, the line connecting the teller (you) and the story is weak because you are not as invested in the story as your manager is. Can you think of a situation where you had to deliver a message you didn't really believe in? One way or another, your lack of belief probably affected how you shared that message, and it subsequently impacted how your audiences received it. If you had zero enthusiasm for the story, then your audience was likely not moved by it either.

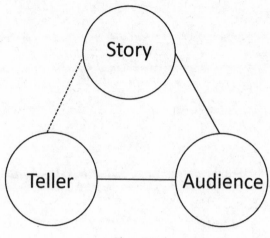

Figure 7-2

Another example. Say you're a big fan of the Kansas City Royals, winners of baseball's World Series in 2015. Your son was barely a year old at the time, and of course knew nothing about baseball. But when he becomes old enough to understand the story, you tell him—repeatedly—how your favorite team won the championship back in 2015. In this case, how the Royals won the World Series is the story, you are the teller, and your son is the audience, as in Figure 7-3.

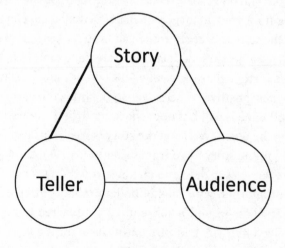

Figure 7-3

Let's further say that at the time of your telling, your son is not yet a big baseball fan (you're working on it!) but doesn't resist the sport either. So the line connecting him and the story is of moderate strength. You, however, have a strong connection with the story (represented by the thicker line in the figure), and this definitely affects how you tell your son the story—with a lot of conviction and enthusiasm, maybe even acting out some of the plays in the baseball games.

Now that you understand the concept of the relationships among story, teller, and audience, let's bring in point of view, sticking with the World Series story. Say that somewhere across town from you are another father and son. The son's about the same age as yours, but his father happens to be a big fan of the New York Mets, who *lost* the 2015 World Series to the Royals. Assuming both fathers stay true to the facts, think about how different the stories they tell their sons about the World Series will be. Each saw the same games, but will emphasize very different things, depending on their point of view. For example, the Royals (winning) fan might talk about how great the team's hitting and fielding was, while the Mets (losing) fan could talk about how some questionable calls by the umpires put his team at a disadvantage.

Point of view is a powerful thing, as any comparison of historical accounts of the same events by different countries illustrates—such as how England and the US tell the story of the Revolutionary War. The idea is that the more stories you collect, the more adept you will be at understanding and speaking from different viewpoints. Like a polyglot who can shift between languages depending on whom she is speaking with, the more stories you collect, the more able you will be to use the point of view that yields you the most persuasive power with a given audience. As you can imagine, speaking from a point of view that matches that of your audience will ensure that your story resonates with them. Story collecting, in this context, is a highly valuable activity.

ACKNOWLEDGMENT IS A WONDER DRUG FOR STORY

Acknowledgment is the invisible energizer that keeps us motivated in many settings and circumstances. "To acknowledge" is generally defined as: 1. To accept the existence of; 2. To recognize the fact or importance of; and/or 3. To show that one has noticed. Tony Schwartz, CEO of The Energy Project, observed that "To feel valued (and valuable) is almost as compelling a need as food."[4] Thus, when we acknowledge others, we are also making them feel valued. But as Schwartz warned in a *Harvard Business Review* blog, "The more our value feels at risk, the more preoccupied we become with defending and restoring it, and the less value we're capable of creating in the world." Therefore, collecting stories will not only help you become a better storyteller in the same way reading helps build writing skills, but it can also serve to acknowledge your audiences, letting them feel heard, understood, and validated.

Because acknowledgment is such a critical piece of point of view specifically, and storytelling more broadly, I offer three brief examples that illustrate this process in action.

Stabilize the patient

I was the baby of my family, the younger of two children. I was also a naturally good listener from an early age, so my family members liked to talk to me about their problems with one another instead of dealing with such conflicts directly. As *de facto* peacemaker and family therapist for nearly twenty years, by the time I entered graduate school in 1996 I was eager to participate in mediation training. I imagined diving into how to handle key stages of dispute resolution, with maybe a little bit of psychology, counseling, and law thrown in.

I was wrong. Those topics were all covered eventually, but at the beginning of the training the leader focused exclusively on what he called the mediator's "first job." It wasn't about any kind of problem-solving, but about taking great care to *acknowledge aloud*—but not agree with—what each disputing party wanted from mediation.

For example, in a mediation between two neighbors in a college town, the woman living next to students who hold loud, late-night parties might want them to move out of their rented house immediately. The students, meanwhile, would like the elderly lady living in the house next to them to stop telling them to be quiet at 8:30 p.m. and calling the police to break up their get-togethers. Such wants, regardless of their validity, must be acknowledged early in a mediation.

"Stabilize the patients," our trainer repeated over and over throughout the certification program. He likened acknowledging each party in mediation to dealing with patients who'd just been admitted to the emergency room. Such patients need to be stabilized immediately, before any diagnostic or treatment procedures. Likewise, what mediators need to do before anything else is to acknowledge each party's desired outcome, however unreasonable or unrealistic. When people are in emotionally charged situations, feeling heard can disarm resistance to change.

Retain a star employee (or not)

One afternoon, my client Bill (not his real name) came to our coaching appointment, and I could tell something was not right. When I asked what was wrong, he told me he'd soon have to find a replacement for his favorite analyst. Steve? Not Steve! (After coaching him for months, I'd gotten to know his team quite well.) Steve was the favorite analyst of Bill and his partner, having started with the company four years earlier as a college intern. In fact, Steve was about to be promoted. Even if they could find someone with a similar intellectual caliber and can-do attitude, it would take years for the new hire to accumulate Steve's level of institutional knowledge and understanding of company culture. Why was Steve leaving when he was about to be promoted, I asked. It turned out Steve *didn't know* about the impending promotion. Sure, he had been well compensated and treated fairly. At this small company, however, Steve couldn't see much opportunity for career advancement, as all the senior people seemed to be staying put. Worse, as Bill and I discussed the situation further, we realized that Steve had never really heard from him or his partner how much they valued him and his contribution. Without perceived advancement opportunity or acknowledgment, Steve decided he needed to go elsewhere to grow.

Elevate corporate culture

Pete Kadens, serial entrepreneur, renewable energy executive, and champion of homeless issues, can recount many achievements and success stories. One of the things he's most proud of is a program he launched at one of his companies. Called "Mad Prop,"[5] the program is a peer recognition system realized as a database to which employees can submit notes of recognition about their colleagues' positive examples or impacts, for public recognition. Anyone can submit a note of recognition at any time, so long as it's substantive (showing up for work on time doesn't count!). An algorithm collects and processes all the submissions, and then a committee reviews them. Everyone within the company can read the submissions, as well. At the end of each month, quarter, and year, employees who've earned the most recognitions win cash prizes.

The system made Kadens's broad employee team feel acknowledged and valued, and it ensured that the hard work of acknowledgment did not fall only on management's shoulders. Everyone in the company was free to offer "Mad Props" to colleagues at any time, triggering a virtuous cycle of reciprocity and enhanced motivation. Thus, beyond the short-term effects of the monetary rewards, Kadens observes that Mad Prop elevated the company's culture for the better, as one marked by frequent, positive acknowledgment.

One of the best ways to acknowledge individuals in any setting is to help them uncover their own stories and listen to them aggressively. Let's talk about ways to do that.

ASK CRAZY GOOD QUESTIONS

"I don't have good stories to tell!" many of my clients lament when we first begin working together. "You do," I assure them (while acknowledging their concern!). "You just need to put on the right pair of story-finding glasses."

When it comes to mining our own stories, our "vision" tends to fail us. Sometimes you can't see your personal narratives clearly because you may have a distorted view of yourself, such as thinking nothing interesting ever happens to you. Others may fail to discern their stories because of short-sightedness, or an inability to look far enough into their experience base. Just as almost no one likes the sound of their own voice, when we think about our own experience, we generally lack the distance, perspective, and objectivity to evaluate what story, if any, is worth telling. People often don't notice a great story that is right in front of them. That means that when you collect stories from others, your job is to see what they themselves can't or won't. In most cases, once you point it out and validate it, they can quickly start sharing meaningful stories.

TEN TYPES OF CRAZY GOOD QUESTIONS

These ten types of questions will help you coax valuable stories from your audience. But they are not meant to serve as a script. Rather, they are a *guide* for how you can help your audience establish the distance, perspective, and objectivity to evaluate their own experiences. You should feel free to improvise, elaborate, and mix and match these question types to mine stories. After the list, I'll present several examples of the questions in action.

1. Origin
- How did [_____] begin?
- What motivated/prompted you to [_____]?
- How did people react to your [_____] in the beginning?

2. Why
- Why do you do what you do?
- [Ask a fact-seeking question], listen, and then ask WHY?

3. Surprises

- What has surprised you the most?
- What has caught you off guard about [_____]?
- What didn't you know about [_____], but wish you did?

4. Compare and Contrast

- How is [_____] different from [_____]?
- What parallels can you draw between [_____] and [_____]?

5. More

- Say more about [_____].
- Tell me more.

6. Meaning

- What does [_____] mean to you?
- What do you make of [_____]?

7. Greatest

- What is your greatest [_____]?
- When are you the most [_____]?
- What and who gives you the most [_____]?

8. Different Path

- How would [_____] be different if you didn't [_____]?
- If you were to take on the role of [_____], how would you handle [_____] differently?
- If you could have any item on your [_____] wish list fulfilled, what might those be?

9. Takeaway

- What are your takeaways from [_____]?
- What did you learn from [_____]?

10. The Self

- How did the experience shape who you are today?
- What does [_____] tell us about who you are?
- When you are not [_____] here, what do you like to do?

The sky's the limit. While these ten types of crazy good questions are great conceptual starts, there are thousands of ways to ask questions tailored specifically to a given situation and conversation. So work with the question *types*, not the specific questions. Then try to be as creative as your imagination allows! The examples below can help.

Project/Strategy Work

One of my clients used to work for an e-commerce company that offered an online community as one of its services/products. Her manager held weekly team meetings where each person would update project status, discuss new ideas, brainstorm, and help create new strategies. Team members would ask many of the Ten Crazy Good Questions of one another during the meetings, as suggested below.

- Why do we do [_____]? (This question helped her team prioritize competing projects.)
- What does [_____] mean to you? (Variations the manager used: What does this product mean to our consumer? Our client? Our sales team?)
- What do you make of [_____]? (Her manager asked this especially when analyzing data.)
- If you can have any item on your [_____] wish list fulfilled, what might those be? (This was useful when her team brainstormed new products/functionality.)
- What are your takeaways from [_____]? (Her team always asked takeaway questions when they wrapped up projects.)

Getting to Know Colleagues

Another client, SVP of a food marketing company, likes to ask his team variations of the Origin, Surprises, Meaning, Greatest, and Self questions, mostly to get to know individual members as professionals and people. This included queries like "What interested you in working in the food industry in the first place?" and "What has surprised you about your work or this company?" This not only helped his team members to feel acknowledged, but also provided him valuable information to determine what projects, roles, and responsibilities fit them best.

Client Needs

One of my clients, a technology consultant, uses the questions to understand her clients' needs and requirements in service of developing the right solutions/recommendations.

- How did people react to your [_____] in the beginning? (He used this question when discussing existing products/functionality or organizational changes; it helped assess change readiness and attitude among the team.)
- What didn't you know about [_____], but wish you did? (This is a good one when looking at existing products and trying to figure out which new functionalities or design would be most beneficial.)

I am a firm believer that it's best not to be overly concerned about impressing others. Instead, let your audience impress you. Let them share their experiences with you and then show them how their experiences, even those they may not find particularly interesting, can be turned into great stories. They will be grateful because you're acknowledging them and helping them understand that they do indeed have great stories to tell.

LISTEN AGGRESSIVELY

Imagine this. You're all set to help your audience mine stories. You've prepared your questions while keeping your mind open to whatever your audience is willing to share. You're ready to improvise. You feel confident that you will collect great stories while helping your audience feel acknowledged.

But despite that positive outlook, once you actually start asking the audience your questions, your mind drifts to what to make for dinner tonight, the client email you need to answer, whether you locked your car, and countless other things that have nothing to do with the task at hand.

So you're not listening.

And you're definitely not collecting stories.

This is why *aggressive listening* is so important. The modern mind gets pulled in too many different directions. For evidence, look no further than the proliferation of meditation trainings, books on mindfulness, and "centering" strategies. A *Time* article suggests that our attention span is now shorter than that of a goldfish: "Microsoft found that since the year 2000 (or about when the mobile revolution began) the average attention span dropped from 12 seconds to eight seconds."[6] There's no question that setting aside our thoughts and worries to focus on what others have to say can be challenging and energy-consuming. That's why we need to be consciously aggressive about listening.

My former boss and retired Northwestern University communications professor Paul Arntson used to say "For every one part talking, do three parts listening." This 75-to-25% proportion of listening to talking is a good rule of thumb. My colleague and fundraising consultant Brian Murphy wants to take listening even further. He likes to share the idea of the "Seven Sacred Channels to the Mind": Two channels through our eyes, two channels through our ears, two channels through our nostrils, and one channel through our mouth. Brian concludes, therefore, that we ought to use them in proportion: That gives your mouth only *one seventh* of the time, even less than 25%!

"True listening is a function of being present to other people's words and meaning," advises fellow storytelling advocate Annette Simmons, "even when, or especially when, their words or meaning might potentially disconfirm or destabilize your own."[7] Clearing your mind for other people's words can be especially difficult if those words "destabilize" your own. So what's the best strategy to make yourself present for other people's words and meaning?

HOW TO LISTEN AGGRESSIVELY

Three empty water glasses? Check. One large plastic bin filled with water? Check. One pitcher full of ice? Check. One tall vase? Check!

Last year I was preparing to speak to thirty-some people about aggressive listening. I'm sure they had no idea why they were looking at a table holding the empty glasses, water-filled plastic bin, pitcher, and vase on the stage. But hopefully they remembered the quote I shared with them early on: "The ability to speak multiple languages is an asset. The ability to keep your mouth shut in any language is priceless."[8]

So, I had all the "props" above on stage with me to demonstrate a simple but powerful phenomenon about listening, using basic physics. I started by filling the vase with water to the brim, then told my audience I wanted to add even more water. I tried using the bin to fill it, but the vase overflowed. I tried using a glass to fill it. Same problem. I tried adding ice cubes one at a time, then dumping multiple cubes into the vase at once, with force.

Nothing worked.

This simple demonstration illustrated a simple truth. Just as you can't pour more water into a vase that's already full, you can't truly listen when your mind is already full—and it tends to be full much of the time, as suggested above. Listening is a prerequisite for collecting stories. And I don't mean just listening for a gap in a conversation so you can talk, listening to develop a counter-argument, or listening simply because it's the polite thing to do.

Aggressive listening is about accepting the idea that a full vase can't take on more water while at the same time doing right by your audience by truly hearing what they have to say. How can you do this? Below are multiple practical, mutually reinforcing tips for being a successful aggressive listener.

Be a film director

Our minds wander. That's a fact. If you've ever tried to meditate, you know how frequently and quickly your mind deviates from a simple task such as focusing only on your breathing. So, when you need to listen aggressively, you can try to create a motion picture in your head as you listen. It may sound strange, but you need to imagine yourself as a movie director, and that your audience has an experience that can potentially be turned into a blockbuster film. Your job is to listen, investigate, and imagine how pieces of your audience's story can be translated into an Oscar-winning motion picture. For example, ask yourself what the setting looks like. If the speaker is describing her cubicle, you could picture a cubicle farm right out of *Dilbert*, with her sitting there amidst her co-workers. If your corporate-team audience is talking about an intimidating sales pitch with a CEO who keeps challenging their numbers, picture the executive's expression and tone of voice. Using your imagination to paint vivid pictures as you listen will help keep your mind on task and maintain your focus on your audience's story.

Listen with your whole body—except your mouth

I have a good friend; let's call her Jane. Jane is the life of the party, someone everyone wants to be around. She is funny and social, a talker who uses her eyes, face, hands, and voice to pull you in and keep you listening, no matter the topic. Jane loves talking and I love listening; we are a great extrovert-introvert match. But the rare times when I'm doing more of the talking, I've noticed a pattern: Jane's gaze wanders and she rarely maintains eye contact; sometimes she bites her fingernails; often she finishes my sentences for me and/or interjects to tell her own story. When she is listening, Jane doesn't display the high level of focus and energy she radiates when she is talking. Of course, it's possible that what I'm saying is truly boring. But given her listening style (or lack thereof), it's easy to imagine that Jane's just not that interested in me or what I have to say. In reality, nothing can be farther from the truth. Jane does care about me—a lot. But I only know that from our history together, not because of the way she listens. And I don't think she realizes that she sometimes gives off this impression of not caring.

To be fair, there's a little bit of Jane in most of us. We all have experience, expertise, and stories to share. But recall from our earlier discussion that the ability to keep your mouth shut in any language is priceless. Moreover, it's important to listen with your whole body except your mouth. Your gaze, in fact, tells more about what's on your mind than any other nonverbal cue. So to listen aggressively, make sure you're looking at the other person most of the time when they are speaking. To avoid inadvertently staring them down, make sure to alternate your focus between the speaker and nearby empty space. Looking into empty space can also be seen as a sign of thinking deeply, which is not a bad thing for a listener (as long as you're thinking about what's being said). Be sure that your arms and legs are not crossed, which might create an impression of defensiveness. For particularly important discussions, a version of *The Thinking Man* pose (leaning forward, hand cupping your chin) can also communicate the right level of care and attention.

Feel what they feel

Body language, however powerful, is not the same as empathy. Professional counselors recognize that clients shut down if they perceive the therapist as judgmental, whether as the result of verbal or nonverbal responses. So the best way to show support and engagement is to really try to feel what your audience feels. Once you grasp how they feel, your head and face can do most of the heavy lifting of expressing that. If the audience you're soliciting stories from sounds angry or frustrated, frown. If they are excited, smile. If they offer a new revelation, nod your head. If they seem confused or confounded, inhale in a deliberate way, hold it for a couple seconds, then exhale slowly. Of course, this should all be done in moderation and without exaggerating the gestures, lest you come across as disingenuous. It works best when you truly feel the emotion you are expressing. But even basic mirroring, in gestures and words, can be powerful. A social psychology experiment, for example, revealed that when a restaurant server repeats customers' orders exactly the way the customer stated them, they can earn up to 70% more tips.[8] Such acknowledgment—the result of aggressive listening—lets the audience feel heard and assures them that the listener is fully present and cares, creating a more satisfying dining experience and greater reward for the listener. You can see how this principle would apply in broader business situations such as listening to clients or negotiation partners.

Ask clarifying questions and paraphrase

There will be times when you are listening aggressively when you feel that something being said doesn't quite add up. Or you may struggle to follow the story. In this case, asking clarifying questions demonstrates that you care about the story and want to understand it fully. Paraphrasing can provide additional evidence. If you can say the same thing in your own words—and more concisely than the original, in many cases—then you and your audience have proof that you've grasped what they're saying. If your paraphrasing suggests that you didn't quite understand, then your audience now has a chance to clarify. In many situations, especially emotion-laden ones, there's nothing more validating than hearing your thoughts, experiences, and feelings expressed in someone else' voice. Just remember to do this sparingly.

Don't interject with your own story

When you care about the story you're hearing, it may be natural for your own stories to come to mind. But try to resist the temptation to interject. The spotlight should remain on the audience, not you. The only exception is if you believe that sharing your story can help your audience gain further clarity or insight, or potentially encourage them to share more openly. For example, if you sense that your audience is hesitant to speak, sharing a small anecdote of your own could prompt them to open up. It is also a good idea to compare your communication preference to that of your audience. If you're an extrovert and your audience tends to be more introverted, it may be hard for you to deal with their longer silences, but it's important not to fill that space, as it may be part of their process of warming up to share. Remember, aim for about three parts listening for every one part speaking. Respect the silence and often the story will follow.

Be curious and respectful

In summer 2006 my husband and I traveled across northern Italy. He spoke a little Italian; mine was limited to "ciao," "grazie," and "delizioso!" Over time we noticed a leafy green vegetable in many restaurants; it looked like rapini, but not exactly. When we finally decided to ask a server about the item, we struggled to be understood (her English was no better than our Italian!), pointing and smiling our way through it. She turned and walked to the kitchen, leaving us confused. But she returned quickly with a plate full of the greens. "Thry, thry!" she urged. Saying "grazie," we dug in. It was delizioso, and she didn't charge us!

That same trip, we lingered around a 17th-century castle in Milan, admiring the architecture. A nattily dressed older gentleman resembling the widower in the Pixar movie *Up* walked out of the front gate. Noticing us, he approached. "Could you tell us more about the building?" we said. He smiled, and in excellent English provided interesting details, including how part of the building had been converted into offices, then asked if we'd like to see the courtyard. Of course! And grazie!

After a few minutes in the courtyard, he invited us to see his office; he was an attorney who'd come in to work on a case that Saturday. His small office was organized neatly and conveyed a sense of grace and dignity. I noticed several black-and-white photos on his desk. In one, people in military uniforms stood near a sheet covering the unmistakable shape of a body. "When was this taken?" I asked, pointing. He explained it was a picture of him and fellow soldiers from World War II, and that underneath the sheet was his fallen best friend. We were stunned and humbled by his generosity and openness.

Worldwide, I've found my respectful curiosity met by openness and even intimacy from all kinds of people. That's the right approach to take to story collecting, as it makes your audience feel acknowledged and cared for. Try it, and you'll find people are very willing to invite you in and show you around, both literally and figuratively.

Practicing the tips in this chapter will help you elicit and collect meaningful stories from a wide range of audiences. Those stories not only deepen your relationship with your audience, as built on mutual respect, interest, and trust, but also give you more narratives to share for your own endeavors.

In the final section of the book, we are going to encounter stories in action, which we can use to introduce ourselves to the audience, to create powerful networking encounters, to support nonprofit causes, and to provide motivation and support in the healthcare industry.

part

THREE

STORIES
IN
ACTION

USING YOUR OWN STORY TO BUILD CREDIBILITY AND CONNECTION

"TELL ME ABOUT YOURSELF."

That simple request comes up frequently in business environments, whether you're interviewing for a job, speaking as part of an expert panel, or just getting to know a colleague or potential client. As innocuous as it sounds, the question strikes fear in the heart of many, as they're unsure of what to say or how it will be perceived.

But it doesn't need to be so scary.

As an introduction to this chapter, let me give you one example of how I approach this question, by telling the story of my early experience as an MBA student at Northwestern University's Kellogg School of Management. In the first weeks of the program, I noticed many classmates smiling and waving at me in the hallways; "Hi, Esther!"

The problem was that I had *no idea* who they were—not their names, not even their faces! I'm not a drinker and I don't have prosopagnosia (the condition where you can't recognize faces), so I figured I'd never met them. Then how did they know me?

A few conversations with my greeters cleared things up: the majority were the people who sat behind me in class (I admit it: I sat in the first row!), and they knew me because I asked a lot of questions.

"Thanks so much for asking that question about calculating net present value the other day," one classmate said. The more people who thanked me for my questions, the more I understood that a *lot* of people didn't understand the lectures.

Ironically, to that point, I'd felt very alone, as if I was the only one drowning in a sea of finance, accounting, and marketing terms—an imposter among people who deserved to be there. At one point, I thought I must be an "admission mistake!"

I was so glad I didn't continue to doubt myself! It turned out so many of my classmates felt just like I did, even though most of them chose not to ask questions. It takes just one person to say, "I don't get it. Could you explain again?" And I was, and still am, that person.

This chapter is about how to respond to "Tell me about yourself" with a story that will help you connect with your audience, so that the next time someone says "Tell me about yourself," you can reply first with "I'm glad you asked!"

THE INEVITABLE QUESTION AND THE LIKABILITY METER

In business settings, hearing "Tell me about yourself" is inevitable, and your answer to it *matters*. Offering a compelling answer will set the right tone with your audience, establish trust and credibility, and increase your persuasiveness.

This is where likability comes in. Psychologist Robert Cialdini's research on social influence shows that not only do we tend to like those whom we perceive as being like us, but we're also more likely to form a stronger connection with them and find their ideas persuasive.[1] Because of this, the "Tell me about yourself" question is actually a great opportunity for you to present ways that you might be like the person asking the question. (My Kellogg story often works in this way, as many people want to ask questions but don't, and appreciate those who do ask questions [within reason!]). I'm not saying you'll always hit common ground, but a strategically crafted answer is more likely to resonate than not.

According to research by Lauren Rivera, an associate professor at the Kellogg School, interviewers give top rankings to applicants who remind them of themselves.[2] So when the interviewer says "Tell me about yourself," what they really mean is "Tell me something about yourself that reminds me of *me*." And if you can do that, you'll be moving the likability needle closer to "I really like this candidate!"

"Reminding me of me" encompasses a wide range of possibilities. For example, aspects of your personality or background, or even your own business-related struggles could remind the interviewer of herself. Say you know from their bio that your interviewer has a colorful, non-linear career history, for instance; you could forge a stronger connection by referring to your own professional twists and turns, presuming you have these and that they still represent a logical path to the job you're interviewing for. Similarly, Rivera talks about how a candidate for an elite law firm formed a deeper bond with her interviewer when she became aware that the interviewer was a single mother and shared her own experience—and gratitude—as a child of a single mother. And it's not only the shared experience but also the shared *story* that creates the bond. When we tell stories in a way that aligns them with narratives familiar to or experienced by the listener, we automatically move higher on the likability scale. The five business-story plots outlined in chapter 2 are a great way to use well-known narrative frameworks as the vehicles for your story, increasing understanding and likability.

Of course likability will serve you well far beyond job interviews. The same principle applies to being chosen as, say, an investment manager, or winning a bid as the *one* new vendor. In such scenarios, again, "Tell me about yourself" is your chance to tell a story that highlights shared experiences and stories. And whether you're looking for a new job, fundraising for a new business, or meeting a new prospective client, telling a compelling story when asked about yourself will help you make a meaningful human connection.

HOW CAN MY STORY MAKE ME
SIMILAR TO MY AUDIENCE?

To increase the odds that someone will find you similar to him- or herself, naturally it helps to find out all you can about that person before you meet. Unfortunately, even with information so readily available online, that's not always possible—especially in situations where you won't even know the name of the person with whom you'll be speaking ahead of time.

So how do you choose a story that you *know* the person will be able to relate to when there's no way to learn anything about that person in advance? First, think about what's universal—that is, things that provoke a "Me too!" response. At the same time, bear in mind that your potential employers, clients, or funders are not interested in merely seeing a mirror image of themselves. So, for example, it's not about finding out, for instance, that the person loves spelunking and bringing up that *you* love spelunking. That might just strike them as a bit stalker-ish. Instead, tell a story about yourself that's universal enough to make them think about how it harmonizes with their own story. For example, if the job involves travel, you might share a story of a recent cross-cultural experience—such as working abroad—and what you learned from it, as a way of finding a theme of mutual interest.

Use any information you can about the person you're talking to— interests they mention, pictures in their office, cultural background, taste in clothing—to determine the best story to deploy.[3] For example, if your interviewer has lots of pictures of sports (or cats), try to tell a sports-related (or pet-related) story. Sometimes the simplest approaches are the most powerful.

For me, raising my hand in classes eventually led me to realize that I was not alone. I had thought my experiences were unique (*I'm the only one who feels out of my depth and doesn't understand all the complex concepts in our lectures*), and I felt isolated and inferior because of that imagined uniqueness. But the thing is, once we voice the experiences we imagine are ours alone, we typically find that our stories are part of a *shared* thread of human experience—a thread that, once identified, can bond us much more closely to others.

THINK IN THREE ACTS

Now let's think a bit more about how exactly to construct your personal story, once you've chosen a specific topic that you think will resonate with your audience. Because one of the great, essential shared-experience narratives involves overcoming adversity or solving a problem, we'll use this story type as our example. Most of us can identify with overcoming some form of adversity to get where we are, and so we love to hear how others have done the same.

To make your story compelling, it's vital to demonstrate that you have surmounted significant hurdles or solved tricky problems on the road to success.

A story with no obstacle isn't much of a story: "I had a problem and I figured it out easily. The end." Boring!

Once you've selected a story that involves significant *obstacles* or hurdles you had to clear, think about the best way to construct the story to resonate most with your audience. The good news is that you don't have to figure out a basic story structure. Remember the Three-Act Formula in chapter 1? You can use this very same structure for your story, taking advantage of all the thinking that has already gone into it. Remember, also, another lesson from chapter 1: the importance of an effective *hook*. In your "Tell Me About Yourself" story, that well-crafted hook turns the audience members into active listeners because they want to hear the story and figure out its message. (See chapter 1 for more on using conflict, contrast, and contradiction to hook your listeners.) A good Act I hook will make your audience anxious to find out what happens in Act II—the middle section and, often, the most complicated part of the journey.

While all three acts are critical, Act III has a lot of work to do. It's your chance to lead your listener to your final point, as related to the specific context you're in. That means you should wrap up your story with: "So that's why I am here. And this is why we're having this conversation." For example, "So that's why I think investing in my venture would be a great opportunity for you" (after you've explained in detail all the obstacles you've overcome to build your venture, and why it's something your audience cares about). In short, your listener needs to understand *why* you are telling this story. Act III is not just a resolution of your story—it puts your story in context and illustrates for your listeners the value that you bring to their situation.

As you construct your story, remember that "less is more," and thus more is often less. Aggressively exclude irrelevant information. How will you know what's irrelevant? You start by finding the narrative theme that weaves throughout your three acts. Without a theme, your story will have no backbone. But once you discover that theme, you can be disciplined in weeding out information that doesn't relate to it. In my Kellogg story, for example, the theme was having the courage to admit I don't understand something, and ask for help so everyone benefits.

Now let's consider a few more specific examples of story-based responses to "Tell Me About Yourself"—stories that exemplify the effective use of the three-act structure.

After each of the "Tell Me About Yourself" stories below, I'll offer a critique to show what works well and what could be strengthened.

WAS IT REALLY THAT SIMPLE?

This story was written by Andy Hick, an asset-management veteran based in Chicago. Andy and I had the opportunity to work on his response to "Tell Me About Yourself" when he was in job transition and preparing for interviews. After crafting a solid "Tell Me About Yourself" story, he was able to transition to becoming a managing director at another firm.

⌒

I was raised in Oak Park, Illinois, and as a high school kid I had a lawn-service business and did odd jobs around our neighborhood. One of my customers was an executive at Kidder Peabody, a Wall Street brokerage firm. He was also the president of the Chicago area Yale University Alumni Club. It was well known that each year, he would offer a deserving Yale student a job at the Chicago Board Options Exchange (CBOE). I wanted that job!

So, a few months before graduating from high school, I called him and asked for the job—despite the fact that I was not a Yale student but was going to the University of Illinois. I got the job and had similar jobs with Kidder Peabody all throughout college—that was my entrée to trading.

My senior year at Illinois, I was interviewing for all types of jobs, but I was really interested in one company: O'Connor & Associates. I had come to know about O'Connor from my summers on the CBOE and Chicago Board of Trade (CBOT), where they were viewed as the "best of the best." O'Connor & Associates was a very successful proprietary option trading firm and was among the first to utilize the Black-Scholes option-pricing model to value options.

I was able to trade interview slots with a close friend who had no interest in trading. I went through an intensive interviewing process and received an offer to join the firm. I was thrilled. I accepted the offer and so began my trading career.

I spent thirteen years at O'Connor & Associates and rose from a "runner" on the floor of the CBOE to a managing director running a multi-billion-dollar over-the-counter equity derivatives trading book.

As I consider my current situation, I think back to those days, and what sticks with me most is the importance of recognizing an opportunity and pursuing it. People generally want to help; but if you fail to ask, the opportunity is not going to come knocking at your door.

Critique of Example 1:

Act I: The opening paragraph is brilliant! This storyteller sets the scene in simple but effective ways, all in eighty-one words!

Act II: In his second paragraph, the storyteller makes it sound like all he did was ask the gentleman for the job and he got it.

My hunch—and maybe yours too—is that the actual process wasn't so simple. Maybe it felt simple now with the benefit of hindsight. But your audience doesn't yet have that benefit. So, bring back the fog. Giving the audience even a slight glimpse of what he actually did would indicate to the listener what obstacles he overcame, giving the audience a deeper appreciation of Andy's character.

Act III: The last paragraph is beautifully done. I can't think of a better way to end. My only recommendation to this storyteller is that he should be sure to link back to *why* he is telling this story—"so that's why I'm here and why I'm well-suited for . . ."—providing closure and moving toward the heart of what he wants to accomplish in the meeting.

Andy could also consider choosing his details differently, depending on his audience. For his target audience when we crafted this story, for instance, mentioning "the Black-Scholes option-pricing model" worked well to establish the speaker's authority. If he were to speak to an audience of laypeople, or a cross-departmental team, he might use other details to establish his authority. It is important to remember that the story is ultimately about your audience, not about you.

WHEN THERE ISN'T AN ACT III

This example is a story told by Stephen J. Dubner, bestselling author of many books, including *Freakonomics,* and host of the award-winning podcast *Freakonomics Radio.* Dubner shared this family-related story as an introduction to a live show he hosted in St. Paul, Minnesota, with his co-author, University of Chicago professor Steven D. Levitt.[4]

⌁

I grew up in kind of a strange family in upstate New York . . . [on a] little farm outside of Schenectady, New York. We were poor. My dad was a newspaper man. We had this little farm with chickens and a large garden. We were poor, but everybody was poor, so it wasn't something you thought about.

Money, even though it was scarce, was not our prime scarcity. Our primary scarcity . . . in a big family, especially me because I was at the bottom of the family [the youngest of eight children], is time alone with a parent. For me, particularly time alone with my father was extremely rare.

I remember one time . . . [my dad] took me into town to a place called Gibby's Diner. . . . [W]e walk in and we sit down at the counter, and I don't remember what I ate, but I remember well what my dad had. He had a cup of coffee with a scoop of ice cream in it. I didn't really think about it as a kid, but now I think that's very clever. You got the coffee; you got the dairy, sweetener, and vanilla all in one pot. My dad was a Starbucks imaginer before Starbucks existed.

So, we're at this counter and we're looking at this mirror. You know the ones diners have. So you can see the whole diner in back of us. He says, "I want to teach you something called the 'power of observation.' It's this game I have.

"What I want you to do is to spend the next five minutes or so just looking around and tak[ing] it all in. I want you to look and listen and smell and just take it all in." I have no idea where my dad is going with this, but it's this wonderful, precious thing and I'm going to do anything he tells me to do. So I do it.

Then after a few minutes he says, "Okay. I want you to close your eyes now." So I close my eyes, and he says, "Okay, the waitress, Ann: what color apron is Ann wearing?" And I say, "White?" And he says, "Aw, come on, you're just guessing." So I say, "White!" And he says, "You're right.

"Since we started this," he continues, "how many cars have pulled into the parking lot? The guy over there, what color shirt is he wearing?" On and on and on. And I am terrible. I have no powers of observation whatsoever. And we do this for a while and it is just grueling and terrible.

So he says, "Open your eyes and we'll start it again." And we do it again and I'm still terrible. We do it over and over and over again. After about twenty minutes, it turned out that I had developed some powers of observation. I learned on that day that memory, or at least observation, is a muscle. You can build it and you can turn it into something. What I do have, by now, is not a talent. But after doing it for so long, [I have] the ability to look around the world and try to see what's happening and try to explain it and write it down. That's all I have, and that's what I do. And the good thing is I love to do it.

Critique of Example 2:

The Likability Meter: Spending quality one-on-one time with parents probably makes it into most adults' top ten favorite childhood memories. That makes Dubner's story here extremely relatable. He also brings us into the intimate conversation he had with his father, which helped him learn the power of observation.

Speaking Context: The context is paramount. Since Dubner is best known for his co-authored books *Freakonomics* and *Super Freakonomics*, thrilling explorations into the "hidden sides of everything" based on economic research, his audience wants to know "How did he come to be so good at what he does?" And this story explains a great deal.

Act I: Dubner opens the scene with the hook of not having much alone time with his parents. He starts with scarcity, an obstacle to be overcome.

Act II: He takes us on this journey of his learning the power of observation, which his father shared with him.

Act III: And then in Act III . . . well, there is no Act III here, other than the general idea that Dubner has benefited greatly from using the power of observation. But in this context, the absence of Act III is okay because the audience deliberately came to see Dubner, as they were already fans. For that reason, reiterating why he and his audience are together in this context isn't necessary. The audience already knows they're there because Dubner has "the ability to look around the world and try to see what's happening and try to explain it. . . ." And since the audience knows why they're attending, he doesn't need to state it explicitly.

In a different context though, one in which Dubner's work was unfamiliar, he might need a brief Act III to make the "So, that's why I'm here and this is why we are having this conversation" connection clearer.

THE BRIDGE FROM PERSONAL TO PERSUASIVE

Kelly Standing is an author, motivational speaker, and speechwriter, among other things. Kelly and I co-chaired the Speaking Society at the University Club of Chicago, where we collaborated on creating opportunities for anyone who wanted to hone their speaking skills, whether in a formal or informal setting. Although as an entrepreneur she doesn't need to interview for jobs, she is often asked by prospective clients to say something about herself. Here is how she responds.

∽

Life has knocked me around . . . a LOT . . . but I'm one of the happiest, most resilient people you'll ever meet. The bumps and bruises started early. When I was six years old, the neighborhood bully used my own jump rope to hang me from a tree by my neck! He left me there to die . . . just dangling, with my little red Keds barely off the ground.

Fortunately, my dad came along and saved me just in time.

I'm sure, at the time, all the typical questions crossed my dad's mind . . . "Who DID this??!" . . . "Where IS he?" . . . "Where's my baseball bat?!" . . . "How quickly can I clobber the kid and hide the evidence?"

But my dad, the Eagle Scout, asked an even better question . . .

a question that would SAVE the day instead of his beating up the bully and making matters worse. My dad asked himself, "How will my daughter remember this?" . . . He forced himself to focus on what REALLY mattered to him in that moment: me.

"Will Kelly see herself as a victim, with a bully hiding behind every tree, waiting to string her up by her neck . . . or will she see herself as strong, resilient, able to handle anything that comes her way?"

That series of questions changed EVERYthing. On that day, my dad convinced me I was the "luckiest little girl on our block." He convinced me that "Your scars make you MORE beautiful, not less so. Your scars tell your story." And over time, in multiple situations, he asked me the same questions he had asked himself that day—"Would I see myself as a victim or a strong, resilient person? What could I learn from challenging or painful events?"—helping me understand that posing the right queries at the right time can literally change people's lives.

From that one episode I learned to ask good questions. Later, I went on to the University of Missouri School of Journalism, where they taught me even more about asking good questions. That's what I do for my clients today . . . I bring a journalist's curiosity and an Eagle Scout's ingenuity to their business problems. I help them tell new stories about themselves. I help them see possibilities where they might see only pain. I help them ask better questions, just like my father did when he found me strung up in the tree that day.

Critique of Example 3:

The Hook: Every parent's worst nightmare is their child being put in harm's way. Here, Kelly brings us directly into a truly horrible incident that happened to her. Yet it was the noble, calm, and superior judgment of her father—and his questions— that turned the plot around. Kelly showed her audience how this frightful event has changed her for the better under her father's guidance.

"That's why I am here and why we are having this conversation": Most importantly, Kelly makes clear at the end of her story how this experience can ultimately benefit her clients. The bridge from a personal event to the value that this storyteller would bring her audience—by asking the right questions—is what makes this story so brilliant and memorable. Thus, the audience will clearly see the link between Act I and Act III.

THE LOWEST NUMBER ISN'T NECESSARILY THE BEST

Near-death at a bully's hands isn't the only way to make your story compelling. Here, a senior energy industry executive named Danny Carlisle and I had a chance to tinker with how he would respond to "Tell Me About Yourself" if he were to meet a new colleague.

⌒

I am the third of three boys, and I'm the only one in my family to have completed higher education. My eldest brother didn't apply, and my middle brother dropped out. My parents were really keen that I make it all the way. I was, in their eyes, their last chance. My dad would regularly say, "You need to study and succeed, so you don't end up doing blue-collar work like me."

This made me both driven and competitive. I wanted to be top of the class. I wanted to win, in exam results and then later, in my career. When I took a role in procurement, I got to run my first global bid, which pitted suppliers against each other. It was a buyer's market and I was able to drive the prices right down. But during the negotiation, my boss gave me some advice. The lowest number isn't necessarily the best for the long term. In any deal, both parties need to feel they won something for it to be sustainable.

This lesson has stayed with me ever since and has become part of my DNA. We negotiate every day in both our personal and professional lives. I want to find the win-win in the situation. By stepping into the other person's shoes, I look to see what success might look like through their eyes. This makes relationships sustainable. Even with my brothers!

Critique of Example 4:

The Hook: In Danny's story we, the listeners, can hear our own. He begins with his birth order and his two older brothers, along with his wish to make his father proud. We immediately think of our own childhood, our siblings (or lack thereof), and how our family life affected us. He effectively and seamlessly sets the stage for why he became competitive and hints at how it isn't necessarily going to be a good thing.

What He Overcame: Although there was no imminent actual danger in Danny's story, we can relate to him because we all owe our start—good or bad—to our family. But he didn't stop there. In his journey of how he eventually course-corrects his competitive attitude, his audience can see a genuine change in his outlook and sense the maturing of a business executive. This ties in well with Danny's introduction because he receives advice from two father figures: his actual father and, later, his manager. If conflict is the nerve center of story, change is the soul of it. Without change, a story feels lifeless and aimless.

That's Why We're Here: We can all appreciate a colleague, a manager, a client, a supplier, a teammate, or a friend who looks for the win-win. How can anyone not look forward to working with Danny?

NOW IT'S YOUR TURN!

It's daunting to stare at a blank screen or sheet of paper in hopes of coming up with a story, so the outline below breaks up what can seem like an overwhelmingly large task into much more manageable chunks. Don't handcuff yourself to the order of Act I, then II, then III. Just fill in whatever parts come to you first. The wonderful thing about mining your story is that when you start with one idea or even just an image, related ideas or memories often follow easily. So the most important thing is to get started, whether you feel inspired or not.

Truth be told, the ending—the take-away—is most important. This is the part where you'd ask yourself this question: "If my audience remembers nothing else about my story, what would I hope he or she takes away?" If you already know what that takeaway is, start with the end. Knowing the takeaway will be hugely helpful when it's time to trim story details, a task most people, even experienced storytellers, find challenging.

Remember: Crafting your story is a *process*, not a destination. So follow the process that works for you, write a draft, test it with your trusted friends and colleagues to act as your mock audience. Ask them to put themselves in the shoes of your actual audience. Ask for feedback and then refine. Repeat the process until you run out of ideas to improve your story, or out of time, or both.

> ## STORYTELLING OUTLINE:
> ## TELL ME ABOUT YOURSELF

Act I: *Setting the Scene.* Begin with a shared experience and end with a hook.

- For an *interview,* when it's likely that you will not be told all the interviewers' names or backgrounds in advance, you may want to favor a positive shared experience over a negative one, while still making it clear that there was an obstacle to overcome.

- When you're *pitching an idea*, select your shared experience based on a character trait you think will highlight your ability to bring the idea to fruition.
- When you're *fundraising*, you may want to focus on a shared experience that can easily be broadened to underscore the importance of giving to your cause, company, or project.
- When you're *meeting a potential client*, choose a story that can move from personal to persuasive (like motivational speaker and writer Kelly Standing's story), illustrating the value you would bring to this client.
- End this act with a hook that has the central challenge embedded in it—like Dubner does when he mentions time with his parents being scarce.

Act II: Describe the journey through which you overcame the main challenge.

- When you're *meeting a potential client*, choose a story that can move from personal to persuasive (like motivational speaker and writer Kelly Standing's story), illustrating the value you would bring to this client. What went through your mind? How did the challenge make you feel? Danny Carlisle tells us that the challenge of having his parents see him as their last chance for one of their children to complete college "made me both driven and competitive."
- Shaping this section for each audience will have to do with what you want to persuade them of at the end. For instance, Danny wants to show that he is driven, but he also wants to show us that he is *fair*. So he sets up the initial character-quality drive, and then he shows how he learned to temper it to create win-wins.
- What action did you take? Danny, for instance, applied himself, aimed to be the top of the class, and then started a career that would allow him to use his drive and sense of competition.

- Was there anyone who helped you along or hindered you? How did you interact with them? Let's look at Danny again. His boss gives him good advice at just the right time!
- Your action taken and your choice of mentioning people who helped you should flow naturally from the shared experience you have chosen, and should also tie back to what you want to persuade your audience to do or think.

Act III: Deliver the resolution and takeaway: why your audience should care.

- What does this journey mean to you and your audience? Danny realized that it's not about the "win" but the "win-win." What this means for the audience is that he negotiates fairly, and this makes him a good leader.
- For an *interview*, you can now highlight how this makes you a good fit for the position.
- When you're *pitching an idea*, you can now show how this story illustrates your ability to deliver on the idea you're there to present.
- When you're *fundraising*, here's where you broaden your story and apply it to the importance of supporting your venture.
- When you're *seeking new clients*, this section is your chance to talk about the value you bring them (take another look at how skillfully Kelly Standing does this in the earlier example).
- What are the main takeaways for your audiences? Danny's takeaway is subtle: he's shared a life lesson that influences what he is like to work with. He wants his audience—his new colleagues—to know that he will work for the "win-win." What do you want your audience to know? What do you want to leave them thinking about?

TEST YOUR STORY

Once you have crafted your story, give it a test drive before you take it out on the road. Tell your story to a friend or colleague and ask them the following questions:

- **What info do you recall from my story?** This question is important, as most of us are inundated with information daily. It's tempting to include as much data in our response as possible. But then, what good will it do if your audience doesn't remember what you just shared with them? On the other hand, people sometimes remember the most random information. So there's no way to find out except going to the sources directly and finding out what has stuck with them, and what hasn't. Once you've collected the feedback, you're much better informed and positioned to refine your stories so people remember the parts you want them to remember.

- **How does my story make you feel?** Remember Maya Angelou's advice, "people will never forget how you make them feel."[5] How has your story made your audience feel? The emotion evoked will probably have a much longer-lasting impact on your audience than anything you've actually said. Does your test audience member feel inspired? Maybe your story reminded her of an experience of her own? Does your friend or colleague feel confused after your test run? Maybe he has already started glancing at his watch and wondering when the conversation with you will be over. Or, does your colleague feel curious? Perhaps he can't wait to follow up with questions that your story has inspired. In fact, encouraging your audience to ask questions is an ideal place to start the post-story conversation, whether in the context of a formal job interview or casual networking. You can ask for this directly, as noted in the next bullet.

- **After listening to my story, what questions do you have for me?** This is the target at which we should all aim: inspiring the right questions in our audience. Maybe the first or second draft of your story hasn't inspired many questions. But shaping it to the point where your audience begins to have questions is a sure sign that you're on the right track. Once you get your audience to wonder more about who you are, it's time to gauge whether the types of questions you prompted lead to the type of topics that you hope to discuss after the initial exchange. For instance, after hearing Kelly's story, potential clients might want to know, "What are some examples of times you brought a journalist's curiosity and an Eagle Scout's ingenuity to a business problem?" Or "This is a current problem we're looking for someone to solve—can you tell us how you might do so?"

The stories shared in the examples section above lead the proverbial horse—the audience, in this case—to water, but they don't force the horse to drink. They don't lay out five points telling the listeners why they should contract with them, hire them, or invest in their idea. Instead, the tellers have told their story in order to inform and influence, with a clear underlying idea of what they want the audience to take away from their stories.

And even though stories are not the same as arguments, you are still telling your story in order to persuade. So, based on your colleagues' feedback, refine your story until it communicates the exact message you want to convey, as indicated by their reactions to the story and questions related to it.

When someone has taken an interest in you and asks you the question "Tell Me About Yourself," you now have all the tools you need to create an enticing and connecting story. What happens, however, before someone is genuinely interested in you and asks you to say more about yourself? Though "tell-me-about-yourself" may not be your favorite question, "what-do-you-do" can be even more challenging. Yet, at networking events most people should have something smart about that. Unfortunately, most don't. The next chapter, which will tell us what to do with "What Do You Do?" will show you how.

CHAPTER 9

SUCCESSFUL NETWORKING STARTS WITH A GOOD STORY HOOK

*T*HERE'S A KNOT IN my stomach and my heart is pumping as if I'm running at a full sprint. But all I'm doing is pacing back and forth, stopping to look in the mirror, adjusting my hair and suit jacket for what feels like the thousandth time. "Hi," I say to the mirror. Then "Hi!" with artificial cheer. "I'm Esther. Esther Choy. I'm an entrepreneur, and. . . ." The words trail off, as if they don't belong to me. The funny thing is, I'm not preparing for any kind of competition or even a job interview. I'm just getting ready to go to a networking event—actually, not even a networking event per se, but a workshop hosted by my alma mater to develop an effective "elevator pitch" at networking events. The elevator pitch is that minute-long memorized paragraph that condenses your entire career history into just a few sentences. "Do I have to go?" I ask myself, thinking back to the countless networking events I've talked myself into going to. With a deep breath, I step away from the mirror and out of the house.

By the time I enter the event room—filled with sharp-looking professionals making small talk at linen-wrapped round tables—I'm still making excuses: "If I leave now, I can get back in time for dinner with my family." But as soon as the program kicks off, I'm thankful. One of the workshop facilitators asks the nearly hundred of us there, "How many of you would rather get poked in the eye than attend a networking event?" Almost all of us raise our hands. I feel a rush of relief, but also curiosity. Why do people hate networking events with such passion?

That question stays on my mind the entire night, even as I'm learning how to refine my elevator pitch. "Did you raise your hand when she asked if you would rather get poked in the eye than network?" I ask as many fellow participants as possible. "Why?" By the end, I've talked to almost half the attendees, probably a record for me at such an event. My informal research uncovered three themes for why people hate networking events so much:

- People feel like they're acting like someone else—taking on a role to present themselves to others.
- People don't know what to say, even if they've spent countless hours creating and practicing their elevator pitches beforehand.
- People feel that such events end up being a waste of time— they don't remember much, and they tend not to gain many opportunities from networking events.

When I get home from that workshop, my husband asks "So, did you come up with a killer elevator pitch?" I tell him I found about a hundred people who dislike networking as much as I do. "Cool! Do you feel like it was a good use of your time?" he asks with a tinge of sarcasm. I tell him it definitely was, because it inspired me to find ways to make networking more enjoyable for myself and everyone else. That's what this chapter is about: how to deal much more effectively with networking opportunities, as encapsulated by the dreaded query "What do you do?"

THE DREADED "WHAT DO YOU DO?"

Many people dislike the idea of networking—and not just the introverts among us.[1] Researchers have even documented that people feel "dirty" after engaging in "instrumental networking," or the type aimed at finding a career opportunity.[2] Despite what I said above, I admit that I don't always dislike networking. Occasionally, I'm lucky enough to meet someone I click with and can talk to without feeling like it's part of an unnatural or even "dirty" interaction. Once in a blue moon, I will meet someone with whom I have a truly genuine, productive conversation, as if I've met a new friend. But what if there was a way to make these pleasant, more-authentic, "true connection" situations happen more often? I believe I have figured out a way, and I want to pass it on to you.

What I've come to understand is that much of the problem with networking interactions is rooted in how they *start*. What's the most common question you're asked the first time you meet someone? Most likely, it's "What do you do?" We ask this question of others to help us quickly categorize them, reducing what could be highly complex information about them on multiple dimensions into an easy-to-understand nugget of information we can process quickly and react to. Most of us do this unconsciously, in part to have something to say/ask during that awkward initial moment of first meeting someone, no matter the circumstance. But by asking that—or answering it in the typical way—we've unwittingly set a trap that dooms most networking interactions to being more or less worthless.

When asked "What do you do?" the vast majority of us answer in a very straightforward way. We may respond with our job title: "I'm a consultant." Or something about our function ("I work in marketing") or industry ("I'm in tech"). Prompted further, we may force ourselves to launch into our elevator pitch. Sure, these back-and-forths seem harmless enough, and they adhere very well to our social norms. In fact, the responses involved are exactly what people expect to hear.

And that's a big problem.

The problem is that when people get what they expect from this kind of social interaction, they also stop thinking and imagining—trying to understand the job you mentioned, imagining what it might look like, and so on. And when they stop thinking and imagining, they stop engaging. They don't need you to fill in the blanks because they can do this for you, armed with even the smallest amount of information. For example, a client of mine runs a family business focused on outsourced payroll services. But she could just as easily be selling fruit or even fruit flies, because as soon as she says the words "family business," people stop listening because they figure they already know what that is, likely some kind of mom-and-pop operation. In reality, some of the largest companies in the world are actually family-run/owned, but that may not fit with most people's images and assumptions.

A quote frequently attributed to Albert Einstein is "Logic gets you from A to Z. Imagination gets you everywhere." Whether or not the great physicist actually said that, it points to the importance of stimulating imagination. So what if we give fellow networking-event participants a gift: the opportunity to use their imaginations? Networking could be much less painful. In fact, it could actually become an enjoyable and productive experience. To do that, we first need to understand the components of a big-picture framework for effective networking.

A FRAMEWORK FOR EFFECTIVE NETWORKING

It can be helpful to have an overall framework for understanding the components of more effective networking—including creating a "pitch" that will pique greater interest, imagination, and engagement in your audience. Below I've listed the elements that go into such a framework.

1. Understand the Uniform Pattern

Although the exact content will differ, there is a fairly uniform pattern to networking interactions, and it's not hard to see. Here's the basic pattern of a networking conversation:

A. "Nice weather we're having, huh?": People typically exchange pleasantries before getting into anything of substance.

This is usually in the form of polite comments about the weather, the event, or the venue.

B. Now I will categorize you: One party moves to categorize the other, usually by asking a question like "So, what do you do?" In the US, this question usually means "What do you do for a living?"

C. Do I care?: Depending on your response, the questioning party will typically ask themselves silent questions including: "Do I get it?" "Is it interesting?" "Does it have anything to do with me?" Their internal responses to those will inform an even bigger question: "Do I want to spend more time with this person?" Most answers fall into these two categories:

- This is someone interesting. I'd like to hear more.
- I'm not interested. I'll move on and try to meet more interesting people.

The key, then, is to engage others' interest in you by engaging their imagination. But how? Just like any good storyteller, you need to plant a hook.

2. Plant a hook

A fishing hook helps you capture a fish. A conversational hook helps you capture the attention and imagination of other people. By planting a hook in the conversation as early as possible, you can transform your audience from passive listeners to active investigators.

Good filmmakers understand this idea and use it to their advantage. Andrew Stanton, the director, writer, and producer associated with blockbuster movies including *Toy Story 1, 2*, and *3, Finding Nemo*, and *Wall-E*, explained a key element of storytelling in his TED talk: "Audiences love to work for their meals. They just like to know that they're doing it."[3] When you approach networking through storytelling, you transform what many people consider a dry, artificial, or even "dirty" experience into fun exploration—for your audience and yourself. As Stanton points out, people enjoy a story that allows them to figure out the message. Your audience becomes an investigator, focused on figuring out what it is you do instead of having data dumped on them. With a well-crafted hook, you are effectively making the audience an active participant in the conversation rather than a passive receiver, even if they're just listening.

So what makes a good hook? You may recall from chapter 1 that a hook is nothing more than a conflict, contrast, or contradiction. Consider the hook in Disney/Pixar's movie *Finding Nemo*: A shark destroys a young fish family, killing the mother and all the unborn baby fish but one (Nemo). "I promise I won't let anything happen to you," the father says to the lone surviving egg. Of course, we all know something will happen to the young fish at some point. But we're left wondering *what* exactly will happen and *how* Nemo and his father will get through it. In the next section, I'll explain how to craft the right hook to plant in any networking conversation.

3. Pre-craft the conversation

Lively dialogue always beats a one-way monologue. Can you recall a lecture or presentation that truly captivated you from start to finish? Probably not! In his well-titled paper "Twenty Terrible Reasons for Lecturing," Graham Gibbs, former director of Oxford University's Oxford Learning Institute, outlined compelling arguments (twenty of them, in fact!) for why lecturing is an utterly ineffective way to convey knowledge and information.[4] A conventional elevator pitch is a one-way monologue—or, effectively, a lecture. So why go that route? Since we understand now that networking conversations follow a reliable pattern and that we can capture our audience's attention by planting a hook, you can use that knowledge to *pre-craft* a much more interactive conversation that motivates audiences to try to figure out what you do—using their imaginations—even as you share information with them. A pre-crafted conversation is basically the script of a dialogue that you are able to create by anticipating how your listeners will respond to your hooks and pauses. In the next section, I will show you how I do this with my own story. You'll also see that I can turn this dialogue into a quick one-voice elevator pitch.

HOW IT WORKS:
MY OWN STORYTELLING APPROACH

How do you ensure that your answer to "What do you do?" is intriguing and delighting? How do you hook your audience from the start?

Here's what I do. When asked "What do you do?" I say "Storytelling." That's it. Though it may seem uncomfortable to pause after one word, think of the pause as the white space in printed material—like in a book or magazine article—that gives people the opportunity to process, react, and ask the questions that matter most to them. So the pause is just as important as the words—or word, in this case—that come before it. After the pause, I usually hear things like: "Storytelling, huh? What does that mean?" or "So you write novels or children's books?"

Let's back up for a second. Recall that we have defined a hook as a contrast, conflict, or contradiction. The hook I use is an example of a contradiction. Specifically, I am contradicting my audience's expectation. Inherent in the question "What do you do?" is the expectation that it will lead to information about you do for a living, professionally—not what you do as a hobby or other pursuit. Because most people consider storytelling a hobby—something one would do with colleagues around the water cooler or with their children at bedtime—I intentionally chose that as the answer to "What do you do?" It contradicts my audience's expectation and makes them wonder if I mean that I tell stories for a living and, if so, how? And that prompts them to seek clarification. At that point they are actively working for their meal, as the filmmaker Andrew Stanton says.

You may be thinking "Wouldn't that response annoy some people who just want to know what you do for a living?" The short answer is yes—but while there is some risk to this approach (and we will touch on that a bit more soon), the benefits of standing out and intriguing people will outweigh that cost in most interactions. The key is to understand that different audiences have different expectations. For some audiences, you don't have to move far from the norm to be considered strange or weird. With others, you have to try really hard to distinguish yourself because they may already be unconventional to begin with. It's part of your job to understand your audience and to adapt your approach accordingly. Sometimes a conventional approach is the safest bet.

Now back to my approach. After I offer the first hook—"Storytelling"—and inevitably prompt clarifying questions and therefore engage the audience's interest, I would say a bit more: "Yes, I do storytelling—storytelling for business." Then another pause. Note that having the discipline to *stop* talking is as important as speaking—too many of us ramble or "listen with our mouths" and fail to give our audience the space they need to react and respond. As you can see, while my second response offers some level of clarification by expanding on the first one, it still doesn't provide the conventional information people expect. My audience now may think "Oh, so you're not a novelist or children's book author, but you're somehow applying storytelling to business." But that leaves them with even more questions: how, when, who, where, and so on. So they typically follow up with things like "Tell me more" or "How does it work?" or "Who do you work with?" I've roped their interest further by making them wonder exactly what my professional world looks like, what role storytelling can play in business (and actually result in payment), and why I'm qualified to do what I do.

At that point, I clarify even further, offering the information they probably expected much earlier: "I work with very quantitative and analytical-minded clients like research engineers, data scientists, and investment managers. I help them weave stories that make sense of the data they deal with and present their ideas to a broad range of audiences, because stories are a much more memorable way to forge deeper and meaningful connections."

So, if you piece together the three parts of my networking conversation, you'll see that it's effectively an elevator pitch about me and what I do—something I could say if there's not much room for back-

and-forth conversation. Here's what it would sound like all together:

I'm in storytelling—storytelling for business. I work with very quantitative and analytical-minded clients like research engineers, data scientists, and investment managers. I help them weave stories that make sense of the data they deal with and present their ideas to a broad range of ideas, because stories are a much more memorable way to forge deeper and meaningful connections.

My approach illustrates the technique of turning your audience into investigators who have to work for information—driven by curiosity—rather than having it dumped on them.

"MY PROFESSION IS BORING!"

At this point, many people in my storytelling workshops would complain: "Fine, but your profession is inherently interesting. That's not true for everyone." Fair point. Shall we look at another example?

Here's an example of how one of my clients handled networking conversations *after* we worked on his approach.

Q: "So, what do you do?"

A: "I'm a real estate treasure hunter."

In some circles, the term "treasure hunter" is used a lot, but not in others. As soon as my client says "real estate," the typical reaction would be "Oh, you're a real estate broker." So pairing "real estate" with an uncommon phrase in real estate circles—"treasure hunter"—is a "mix-and-match" technique that creates a hook by contradicting the audience's expectations. Here's how the conversation might proceed:

Q: "Do you buy and sell real estate?" or "Are you a broker?" or "What do you mean by treasure hunter?"

A: "I work with a team to take advantage of inherent cycles of the real estate market to create value for our clients."

Note that just like in my own example, he clarifies a bit, but leaves space for more questions. In response to a follow-up question like "How do you do that?" the answer would be: "Well, most people know that you should buy low and sell high, including for real estate, but very few people understand what that means, let alone how to do it. My firm is a real-estate-focused hedge fund that uses data and innovative modeling to guide us to where the market is truly going. That's how we've been able to generate 22% annualized returns every single year for the past eleven years—the result of successful treasure hunting."

CREATE YOUR BEST RESPONSE TO "WHAT DO YOU DO?"

Now that you understand how to pre-craft elevator conversations, let's work on yours.

Try this: Write your own first response to "What Do You Do?" Be sure to include a hook. Then, write a few possible follow-up questions you might be asked, and then an appropriate second-level hook—you can refer back to the examples above if that will help, but I've also provided additional ones below. Next, write secondary follow-up questions and possible responses. The third response would be the crux of what you do, or what the audience probably expected you to say in the first place. Below are some tips to guide you.

The first hook is usually the hardest to create. Here are three principles and examples to help you create your hook:

1. Create a vivid image

- "I stand between people and prisons." (Criminal defense lawyer)

- "I protect audiences from boring speakers." (Speechwriter)
- "I catch terrorists with spreadsheets." (Risk-management consultant)

2. Use a concrete object and/or action-oriented verb
- "I build financial roadmaps." (Financial planner)
- "I'm a digital revenue generator." (Website designer)
- "I unpack brains." (Corporate strategist)

3. Pair words or ideas that don't usually go together
- "I'm a habit destroyer." (Leadership or life coach)
- "I'm an idea architect." (Social innovator)
- "I help keep the Internet free." (Online marketer)

Definitely flex your creative muscles as you work on this. But remember: an answer that sounds *too* strange will elicit a negative reaction and send your listener to the nearest exit. You have to find that happy medium so that people are intrigued by your first response, may get some inkling of what you do, and want to learn more. The sample responses above are aimed at this middle ground. As mentioned earlier, knowing your audience is key to gauging their receptiveness to this approach. Some deeply conventional types just won't get it, even the most basic versions of it, so don't go there if you sense that's the case.

THE CAREER MATRIX

When pre-crafting your elevator conversation, the top questions in mind should be: "What is it about what I do that my audience is most interested in?" and "What would intrigue them most?"

To help you do that, consider where your career belongs on the following matrix, as seen in Figure 9-1.

Storytelling takes on nuances, depending on the goal of your story. The matrix could help you clarify the goal of your story (see the boxes in Figure 9-1) based on where your career belongs, and you can use

What do you do?

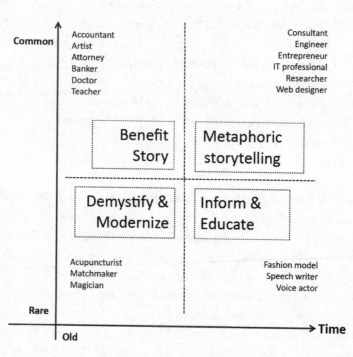

Availability

| Common | Accountant
Artist
Attorney
Banker
Doctor
Teacher | Consultant
Engineer
Entrepreneur
IT professional
Researcher
Web designer |

Benefit Story | Metaphoric storytelling

Demystify & Modernize | Inform & Educate

Acupuncturist
Matchmaker
Magician | Fashion model
Speech writer
Voice actor

Rare

Old → **Time**

Figure 9-1

that knowledge in conjunction with the three principles discussed above. Now let's consider each of the four categories in the matrix.

Common "old" careers

These are conventional occupations with a long history, such as accountant, artist, attorney, banker, doctor, and teacher. If your career falls into this quadrant, the goal for your story is to communicate the core of the value you offer by telling a *benefit story.* An artist could say "I bring beauty into homes and public places." Creating art is what they do, but the true benefit to others is the beauty delivered. A private banker might open with "I'm a confidant" or "I'm a financial confidant." Of course this profession requires a great deal of financial, analytical, and quantitative capability, along with the skills to attract and retain new clients. But all of that is about the banker, not their audience. A better response, again, is about the benefits others experience, which takes the form of a partner who can help them with their financial needs, in confidence.

Reorienting your response around the benefit is a great way to intrigue your audience. This is especially true in this category because people tend to think they know exactly what you do once they hear your profession. So rather than saying "I'm a doctor," a radiologist might say "I use images to save lives." For common longstanding careers, the benefit gives the audience something to relate to and ask about.

Common new careers

Careers that have arrived on the scene more recently include engineer, entrepreneur, consultant, IT professional, researcher, and web designer. So the goal of your story here is usually to create a *metaphor* that allows the listener to understand what you do by comparing it to something more easily understood.

For example, one of my IT engineer clients answers "What do you do?" with "I'm the invisible man everyone needs." When prompted further, he says "I make sure digital communications are unified and clear." Finally, he can explain: "Well, nowadays technology touches every facet of our lives. So we need to make sure all facets work well together. I make that happen by engineering software to integrate phone apps and computers to make sure that communication channels are clear and unified within my company." That helps the listener relate more closely to what an IT engineer of this type does.

Rare "old" careers

Rare careers that have been around for a long time include acupuncturist, magician, and matchmaker. While these fields are sufficiently interesting in their own right, your goal if you happen to work in one of them is to *demystify and modernize* what you do so your audience can understand how it applies to people's lives in the present day. So an acupuncturist might say "I needle people to solve their problems." A matchmaker might respond "I prevent broken hearts." These responses modernize and demystify (with the demystification coming with the fuller explanation), while also pointing to the benefits of the profession.

Rare new careers

Other rare professions that are newer include fashion model, speechwriter, and voice actor. If your career fits into this quadrant, your goal is to *inform and educate* your listener about a field that may be unknown to her or him, at least beyond a superficial level. Most careers in this quadrant are intriguing enough that the listener is eager to learn more.

A great example of a storytelling response for a person in this quadrant is the speechwriter who says "I protect people from boring speeches," as noted earlier. Meeting a speechwriter for the first time, people are likely to follow up with "Wow! How do you become a speechwriter?" or "Have I heard a speech that you might have written?" or "What do you actually do?" Similarly, a fashion model might intrigue listeners and illuminate a subtle element of his or her career by saying "I'm a human mirror." Both the speechwriter and fashion model could then get into more specifics of their careers, and how these might differ from the stereotype the audience may have in mind. For example, some speechwriters may talk about how they work closely on nonverbal aspects of public speaking (hand gestures, eye contact, and the like), rather than the words alone.

We have covered a lot of ground in this chapter, and hopefully you have a better idea of how to deal with the dreaded "What do you do?" The main idea is to understand the uniform pattern of networking conversations and to find a more creative, intriguing way to present your profession, using a hook that encourages the audience to learn more. Don't be discouraged if it takes you some time to craft the right elevator conversation. Many of my clients try out multiple ideas—yes, including in real-life situations—before arriving at the right approach that inhabits the middle ground between intriguing and annoying. So give yourself some space to experiment, think about what's most interesting and beneficial about what you do, and pre-craft the conversation. Ultimately, your audiences will guide you to craft your best story. This is true in a networking setting; this is true in *any* setting!

In the next chapter, we explore storytelling in another setting: the world of nonprofits.

CHAPTER 10

SELLING THE SOCIAL IMPACT OF NONPROFIT ORGANIZATIONS WITH STORY

I WAS THRILLED TO HAVE two ministers at my story workshop in the summer of 2015. They worked with a religious organization that had a chapter at the University of California, Santa Barbara, my alma mater, and their compassion and calm demeanor really helped people open up during the workshop. After one session, I approached them, interested in learning about their organization, possibly to contribute. "Tell me," I said: "what is your organization all about?"

Smiling, they launched into their nonprofit's history, including leadership succession, followed by a laundry list of current programs. Along the way, they debated details, correcting each other politely, almost forgetting their audience (me). Time passed quickly, and as I walked away from them to start the next session, I realized I still had little idea what their organization was about or how I could help.

Admittedly, their only mistake was taking my question too literally by telling me what their organization was all about. The reality is that in today's time- and attention-constrained world, people don't want to know it all, at least not in the beginning and certainly not in one sitting. They want to know whether what your nonprofit does will

resonate with them. So you need to be able to tell your story suc-
cinctly, with impact on the target audience.

This chapter is aimed at nonprofit executives, fundraising professionals, board members, and the millions of volunteers who care
deeply about their causes and want to help raise money, resources,
and awareness for their organizations using story. But the ideas here
apply to anyone seeking to enhance their storytelling impact.

YOU'RE THE BEST—AND THE WORST

You're the champion and motivator behind your nonprofit and know
everything about it. So you're the best teller of its story, right?

Not so fast.

You're likely also the *worst* storyteller.

Why?

Because caring and knowing so much about something makes you
more likely to share all the reasons you care and everything you know.
But to attract, engage, and grow your support and donation base effectively, you need to be highly strategic about what you say, when
you say it, and how you say it. Those two wonderful ministers at my
workshop could've recruited me as a supporter had they not lost me
to the details.

In this chapter, you'll learn how to leverage the tools and frameworks covered throughout the book to tell compelling nonprofit stories, using multiple rich examples, including three fully developed
ones at the chapter's end. You will also see the template that I've developed specifically for telling social impact stories using many of the
tools and frameworks discussed in previous chapters.

Let's say you had an extra thousand dollars to donate to nonprofits
this year. How would you go about deciding which organization de-
serves a share of that? For most of us, the answer isn't clear, partly because what we hear from nonprofits isn't what we're looking for. A 2016
survey showed that 44% of 150,000 donors surveyed said that they
could afford to give more if they heard the right things from
nonprofits.[1]

So what are donors hoping to hear?

THREE PRINCIPLES FOR NONPROFIT STORYTELLING

The answer to the question above involves three interrelated principles for nonprofit storytelling:

1. **Start with their point of view, not yours:** Prospective supporters want to relate to the point of view of your story based on who *they* are, not who you are, so start with that.
2. **Use the "identifiable beneficiary effect":** They want to learn about an individual they may be helping, not just statistics, so give them that.
3. **Direct result, direct impact:** They want to understand and see the direct return on their investment of time and/or money, so make sure to tell them that.

The sections below provide more detail on each of these principles.

Start with Their Point of View, Not Yours

Most nonprofits operate with fewer resources than needed. So they're not that different from for-profit startups and can make use of principles that apply to these early-stage businesses. Serial entrepreneur and bestselling author Eric Ries tells aspiring app designers to stop asking why people don't use their product and to focus instead on why people do use it.[2] It turns out that such users often stick with the product for unexpected reasons.

For example, Kevin Systrom, co-founder of the wildly popular picture-sharing app Instagram, reflected in a podcast that the earlier version of the app was mostly a way for users to check on their friend's locations. But they soon realized that users valued something else much more: the public picture-sharing component. So Systrom and his co-founder scaled the app into what became a $1 billion picture-sharing venture with 500 million active users as of mid-2016.[3]

In the same way, crafting a succinct, effective story for your organization requires you to truly understand the point of view of your most loyal volunteers, donors, and board members. Recall that chapter 3 emphasized the importance of leveraging point of view in your storytelling. If you can relate your story from the most compelling point of view, you're fully amplifying its impact. But wait, you may say, I already know that my most committed supporters believe in my organization's mission—isn't that enough? That may well be true, but you still probably don't know how to tell an organization's story from *their* point of view, which will maximize its impact on them and on prospective supporters with similar perspectives.

So start your storytelling process by mining the point of view of your supporters. Interview some of your most ardent donors or partners, using these questions as guidelines:

- When, how, and why did you get involved with this organization? (It's okay if you know some of the answers, but let them say it in their words.)
- Why have you stayed involved?
- What aspects of your involvement have been most rewarding? Why?

Their initial answers might be brief or superficial, as they may not have thought about the issues much before. So be sure to ask follow-up questions or to reframe the original ones. If your interviewees don't need much prompting, then listen aggressively (see chapter 7), especially for unexpected insights or information. You can also supplement these three key areas of inquiry with the Ten Types of Crazy Good Questions from chapter 7.

An acquaintance who leads an education-focused nonprofit used this approach to interview several supporters and discovered that they found the few opportunities to interact with youth beneficiaries to be the most rewarding aspect of participation, much more than the glitzy annual gala or other events. So she looked for ways to make such interactive events more frequent.

Do your own mining to uncover and harness the points of view of your supporters.

Use the Identifiable Beneficiary Effect

Nonprofit organizations are never aimed at serving just one person. Many measure their impact in units of thousands or even millions served. So it might be tempting to think you can sway supporters merely by touting your large, rising number of beneficiaries.

Actually, in this case it's usually much more effective to talk just about one. Social psychologists describe the Identifiable Victim Effect, or the idea that "society is willing to spend far more money to save the lives of identifiable victims than to save statistical victims."[4] A quote from Russian dictator Josef Stalin illustrates the concept starkly: "The death of a single Russian soldier is a tragedy. The death of millions is statistics." Think about the Syrian civil war that has been ongoing since 2011. After years of devastation, nearly five million people displaced, and daily news coverage of refugees fleeing their homeland with their children in their arms, it was the simple picture (amongst a handful of similar images) of a single blood-soaked, dust-covered child sitting in shock that captured the world's attention—and empathy.

So using the Identifiable Victim Effect—let's call it the Identifiable Beneficiary Effect—is about making your nonprofit story *personal* to elicit greater empathy. How to do that? First, it's interview time again. This time, select a client your organization has served or, in some cases, a volunteer. You want to be able to describe the person well, along with how and why their life intersected with your organization. How does their experience and transformation epitomize what your organization is all about? In the process of story-mining, pay special attention to how the person changed—the before and after—to highlight your nonprofit's impact. The examples at the chapter's end illustrate how to use the Identifiable Beneficiary Effect well.

Direct Result, Direct Impact

As you write your social-impact story, keep in mind that even though reality is laced with nuance, your audience will want a clean, clear storyline that connects your nonprofit's efforts to specific, measurable results. If A, then B.

Say your nonprofit helps children with eyesight issues or kids recovering from eye surgery, like little Johnny, who had a corneal transplant. So, rather than claiming full responsibility for Johnny's recovery, focus on where your organization had *direct* impact. Maybe Johnny had a hard time catching up with his schoolwork post-surgery, so your nonprofit sent a high-quality coach and mentor who helped him use a different learning approach, one that relied less on his vision. As a result, Johnny's grades improved dramatically.

In short, your story needs to focus on the direct results and impact of your nonprofit's efforts, to motivate supporters.

THE SOCIAL-IMPACT STORY OUTLINE

Now that you know three key principles for crafting effective social-impact stories, you can use them in combination with the Social Impact Story Outline to get your story down, especially the all-important first draft.

Based on our trusty Three-Act Formula (see chapter 1), I've created the outline below to help you identify the best information for you to use from your story-mining and other research. Afterward, I've included three nonprofit story examples developed using the outline. These are fictionalized accounts—not from my client work—but based on real, public information from the organizations' websites. Each story is preceded by a fact sheet, a one-page document that every social-impact organization should use to help potential supporters learn about the nonprofit and how they can help.

SOCIAL IMPACT STORY OUTLINE

ACT I:

Begin with a scene, a setting your audience can relate to, such as a time or place; end with a hook.

- Introduce your protagonist (program participant).
- Describe a clear challenge that the protagonist faces, related directly to the organization's mission.
- End with a hook.

ACT II:

Describe the journey through which your protagonist—with the help of your organization—overcame the main challenge.

- Tie the protagonist's challenge in immediately with a larger systemic problem by citing facts or statistics.
- Introduce your organization and how it is uniquely positioned to solve this systemic problem. This should be high-level and succinct.
- Show proof: share metrics that demonstrate your organization's success and/or untapped potential. Include major awards and recognition.
- Circle back to the protagonist and how your organization has helped him or her overcome the challenge.
- Describe how the protagonist's present situation is different—better—because of your organization's efforts.

ACT III:

Provide the story's main takeaways for the audience.

- Ask your audience to imagine a different world, one with real results your organization helps create with your audience's support.
- Make the specific ask. Be realistic.
- Rather than focusing only on the end goal, persuade your audience to take immediate next steps that will support this goal.

EXAMPLE 1:
FLORIDA OCEANOGRAPHIC SOCIETY (FACT SHEET)

Our Mission

"To inspire environmental stewardship of Florida's coastal ecosystems through education, research, and advocacy."

About Florida Oceanographic Society

"Since 1964, Florida Oceanographic Society has worked to protect our coastal ecosystems through education and research. . . . Florida

Oceanographic Coastal Center is a 57-acre marine life nature center located on Hutchinson Island in Stuart, FL, situated between the Indian River and the Atlantic Ocean. As a leading state and nationally recognized environmental organization, Florida Oceanographic offers educational programs to people of all ages and conducts research and restoration programs that lead to healthy coastal ecosystems."

How You Can Help

$30—Buys a dip net for collecting specimens.

$55—Buys a 10-gallon fish tank used for research and education programs.

$190—Provides a scholarship for a child to attend one week of Coastal Discovery summer camp.

$200—Provides instruction, supplies, and take-home activities for 35 students.

$500—Pays for one day of keeping our visitor center and all of its programs open.

$525—Pays for caring for all of our animals for one day.

$2000—Sponsors a paid, full-semester internship.

$3500—Pays for one week of all of our research and restoration projects.

EXAMPLE 1:
FLORIDA OCEANOGRAPHIC SOCIETY (STORY)

Act I

That Saturday in Jensen Beach, Florida was the kind of night that makes you drip sweat even when you're standing still. At Mulligan's Beach House Bar and Grill—the busy hub of a cluster of beach-town shops and restaurants—server Rorie Brakely wished she *could* stand still, instead of bustling about the restaurant taking orders.

Rorie was dumping empty oyster shells from dinner plates into the trash when Donna, a regular customer, walked over. "So you just throw those away?" Donna said, waving a hand at the shells.

Rorie didn't realize that this simple conversation would be her call to action, the start of a very meaningful opportunity.

Act II

That night, Donna told Rorie she'd been volunteering at the Florida Oceanographic Society to build an oyster-shell reef out of recycled shells from local restaurants. "Would Mulligan's be interested in donating their shells?" Donna asked.

Rorie was skeptical initially, and had many questions: Why were people building reefs? Could oysters survive on manmade reefs? How did this help the ocean? Once Rorie finished her shift, Donna explained that growing oyster larvae and releasing them onto the handbuilt reefs was working, as researchers found that the young oysters thrived. The oysters, in turn, cleaned the water and provided habitats or food for crabs, jellyfish, and other marine life.

Convinced, Rorie mentioned the project to her supervisor the next day, and Mulligan's began to donate their oyster shells. Soon, Rorie drove to the FOS Coastal Center and started bagging oyster shells alongside other volunteers.

By the end of the next summer, FOS had worked with restaurants like Mulligan's to save over 25 tons of oyster shells from landfills. With the help of 1,800 volunteers like Rorie and Donna, FOS turned restaurant "trash" into 50,000 square feet of living reef.

Act III

This was just one recent project at FOS. There's much more to do. We need your help for the many challenges facing Florida's beaches and global marine life. We'd be so grateful for your help funding the costs of operating our research and education facilities, running educational summer camps for youth (including those in need), helping citizens advocate for the health of their waterways, and restoring habitats in places like the Indian River Lagoon, home to 36 rare and endangered species.

Our current need for a major gift starts at $30,000. We would be honored to offer you a tour of our Coastal Center and help you learn more. Would you like to invest in Florida's coast, and help the world's "life support system," our oceans?

EXAMPLE 2:
ONERUNTOGETHER (FACT SHEET)[6]

Our Mission

"The mission of OneRunTogether is to financially and spiritually benefit local cancer patients."

About OneRunTogether

Many organizations help pay medical bills, but OneRunTogether assists with the many expenses that overwhelm a family when they face the steep costs of cancer treatment. We pay medical bills and living expenses, including mortgage, rent, and utility bills; childcare while the patient undergoes treatment; and automobile repairs so the patient can travel to doctors' appointments.

Vernon Murphy founded OneRunTogether after his wife, Beth, passed away from breast cancer in 2009, at just 46.

We raise our funds through races and community events. From August 2011 to August 2016, we've made 200 grants, for a combined total of over $62,000.

How You Can Help

- $30—Buys approximately 900 feet of caution tape to mark the racecourse.
- $50—Buys bottled water for over 300 runners.
- $175—Pays for chip timing for 50 participants (includes all equipment, all data entry, and one finish-line manager).
- $350—Pays for chip timing for 100 participants.
- $600—Provides breakfast for 100 runners.
- $1000—Provides race t-shirts for 100 runners.

EXAMPLE 2:
ONERUNTOGETHER (STORY)

Act I

For Reading, Pennsylvania, resident Sylvia Lewis, that July day in 2013 started with another round of chemo for her breast cancer. That much she'd been prepared for. She'd known to ask her oldest daughter, Kari, to drive her to the appointment. She'd known she'd have to spend days in bed, recovering.

But here's what they don't tell you about cancer. It's not *just* the diagnosis, treatment, and recovery. It's dealing with all the other mundane details when you're in real pain. It's standing on your driveway in 90-degree heat, like Sylvia did that morning, leaning against the minivan with your whole body aching while your teenage daughter tries to get the engine to turn over. And it's not *just* medical bills. It's medical bills plus your mortgage, utility bills, insurance payments, and the unexpected cost of a new minivan starter. And so much more.

Act II

One bright spot is how much people care. You expect people to be sympathetic, even to help out a bit, like your children do. But you don't expect to meet people who do *much more* than care, even if they don't know you personally.

That afternoon, after a fitful nap, Sylvia woke up to the phone ringing. It was Vernon Murphy of OneRunTogether. "We've reviewed your grant application," he told her. "Good news: we're going to take care of your next two mortgage payments."

Vern told her his own story: How his wife, Beth, had passed away after battling breast cancer for nine years; how he started running as a way to deal with his grief; how running gave him the idea to start OneRunTogether. He'd been inspired to organize races to pay bills for folks like Sylvia. He asked her if he could visit her and her family, and he arrived the next week, a mortgage check in hand.

That was three years ago. In 2016, Vern came to Sylvia's house with another check, this time for Kari's college tuition for the upcoming semester.

Act III

Sylvia is one of 200 cancer patients OneRunTogether has helped in two Pennsylvania counties. We need your support so we can assist more patients like her and expand into neighboring counties. We'd love your support funding the cost of organizing a OneRunTogether race season, so that all registration fees go directly to patients like Sylvia.

Our current need for a major gift starts at $10,000. We would be honored for you to attend a race and learn more about our organization. Please take a moment to think about how your investment can make day-to-day life less overwhelming for cancer patients like Sylvia.

EXAMPLE 3:
SOS CHILDREN VILLAGES ILLINOIS (FACT SHEET)[7]

Our Mission

"At SOS Children's Villages Illinois, we build Villages that unite brothers and sisters in foster care, surround them with a community of hope, and help them grow into caring and productive adults."

About SOS Children's Villages Illinois

"SOS Children's Villages Illinois offers an innovative approach to traditional foster care. Our model of care gives children the opportunity to live in a nurturing, stable, single-family home with their brothers and sisters in the care of a full-time, professionally trained Foster Parent in one of our Villages. Children benefit from the stability of remaining with their siblings as well as the support of neighboring SOS Illinois Foster Parents and the entire community.

Each Village offers comprehensive services, including: individual and group counseling, mentoring, and educational and cultural enrichment opportunities. This highly supportive setting provides children a sense of safety, security, and community, encouraging them on their journey toward healing and reaching their fullest potential."

In Illinois, SOS Children's Villages operates four sites: three long-term and one short-term residential.

SOS Children's Villages Illinois is part of SOS-Kinderdorf International, "the largest non-denominational child welfare organization in the world with more than 73,400 children living in over 550 SOS Villages in more than 130 countries. More than 1.2 million children and adults are benefiting from various social services provided by SOS-Kinderdorf International."

How You Can Help

$50—Provides a foster child with a complete set of school supplies, including calculator, lunchbox, backpack, notebooks, and more.

$75—Sends one foster parent to a training symposium on youth and mental health.

$250—Provides winter gear for five children.

$500—Enables an entire SOS Village to enjoy a night out at the circus.

$1050—Allows every parent in one of our villages to attend a training symposium on youth and mental health.

$2,140—Pays for two weeks of summer camp at Manito-wish for a foster child.

$4,455—Pays for four weeks of summer camp at Manito-wish for a foster child.

EXAMPLE 3:
SOS CHILDREN VILLAGE ILLINOIS (STORY)

Act 1

Imagine becoming a parent when you're only five years old.
That's what could have happened to Jake.

Act II

Jake is the oldest of three children in the Chicago area. Two years
ago, he was living in a shelter with his 3-year-old sister Kate and
1-year-old sister Lily. His parents, both developmentally delayed,
were unable to provide adequate care. So Jake had to help care for his
sisters, both of whom had significant speech deficiencies. Just a child
himself, how was Jake supposed to be a parent?

Luckily, he didn't have to.

For over 60 years, SOS Children's Villages has been dedicated to
raising orphans and abandoned children in 130 countries, including
many kids like Jake. Currently we have 456 Villages around the
world. In Illinois, our children stay with their brothers and sisters in
an SOS single-family home in one of our Villages, under the care of a
full-time, professionally trained foster parent.

During their two years at the SOS Village, Jake, Kate, and Lily
stayed together as a family, all their needs—emotional, medical, physical, and educational—met by their foster parent and a team of counselors. The children were also able to maintain a relationship with
their biological parents and built a loving, trusting bond with another
relative who ultimately took them into her care when they were
ready to leave their Village. Jake and his sisters are now thriving because they received the care all children should have.

Because of our work, SOS Children's Villages has been nominated
for the Nobel Peace Prize 14 times. In 2012, SOS Illinois was one of 15
Chicago-area charities to be awarded *Chicago Magazine*'s "Gold
Standard."

Act III

No child should have to become a parent for their siblings. To help the too many other children like Jake, Kate, and Lily, we would be so grateful for you to help fund the costs of supporting full-time foster parents, and running educational programs for foster parents and their children.

Our current need for a major gift starts at $20,000. With supporters like you, children like Jake and his siblings have the chance for a supportive home and a brighter future. Would you like to be their champion?

The best way to share your social-impact story is to be selective with details and strategic with content, and to see things from your supporters' and beneficiaries' point of view. I hope this chapter gives you the right tools to tell the most effective social-impact story you can.

In the final chapter of the book, I offer a close-up look at an industry where stories are vital in offering hope, clarity and inspiration.

CHAPTER 11

CASE STUDY: THE HEALTHCARE INDUSTRY

*I*F YOU OWN AND operate a human body, you're involved in health-care. Everyone has interacted with the healthcare system in some form, whether dealing with our own health issues or those of relatives or friends. That means everyone has a healthcare story, and many of these are high-stakes, with large implications for both physical and financial health.

Modern healthcare is immensely complex, and not just for patients. Even people directly involved in the industry their entire careers still only understand a small portion of it. An ICU nurse doesn't need to understand exactly how reimbursement works. A billing specialist needn't be an expert on hospital-acquired infection. A frontline salesperson for healthcare software may know little about academic medical research. But there's often a need to communicate within and across healthcare borders, and storytelling is one of the most effective ways to do this.

Sometimes this means patients communicating with other patients. Here, the growing field of narrative medicine has been critical in helping healthcare organizations and professionals incorporate patients' stories into their work, for greater impact.[1] For example, in

2016 Massachusetts General Hospital launched a Sharing Clinic where patients can share their medical journey through recorded stories. The narratives are stored digitally, categorized, and tagged to help other patients use the interactive listening booth to find stories that inspire, guide, and comfort.[2]

Modern healthcare also has countless specialties, each with its own language, with terms more esoteric as the degree of specialty rises. That only increases the difficulty of creating effective communications for targeted audiences. Story can be a powerful remedy to this challenge.

In this chapter, I will share examples of how five healthcare executives have used the power of story to explain, motivate, and lead. Each story has a different theme and objective. But all share the quality of informing and inspiring others through the use of narrative.

EXPLAIN WHY YOU DO WHAT YOU DO

According to the old adage, people don't care how much you know until they know how much you care. That's certainly true in healthcare, where professionals often derive personal reward from their work, not just a paycheck. Yet, we can't simply *tell* others we care. We must *show* it. And the best way to show how much you care is by telling a story of why you do what you do.

Maureen Blossfeld is a healthcare architect. She designs medical facilities that bring together people, workflow, and materials not only to maximize efficiency but to enhance collective experience. How did Blossfeld get into this highly specialized line of work? Like many, she found her professional calling at the intersection of chance and personal circumstance.

When Blossfeld began her architectural career in the 1990s, she saw her main role in design as creating beautiful, awe-inspiring buildings. Her first healthcare assignment in 2005 completely altered this viewpoint. For that client, a major Chicago-area hospital, Blossfeld's role was to redesign a radiology room. As she toured the radiology department, she came upon the patients' changing room adjacent to a procedure space. The sight took her back several years, when she and her husband sat in a different hospital's changing room, waiting for his diagnosis. They'd prayed for a negative biopsy result. But it was positive, and her husband had succumbed to nasopharyngeal carcinoma, a rare head-and-neck cancer, just a few months before the Chicago assignment.

In fact, the hospital client was her first after her husband's death. Overwhelmed by emotion on that tour, Blossfeld thought briefly of avoiding healthcare-related work altogether. Instead, she decided to devote herself to creating spaces that would enhance the experience of patients, providers, and others, including in their most difficult times.

Once Blossfeld immersed herself fully in that client's facility redesign, she realized such work was a wonderful opportunity to use all she'd learned over the years she'd lived and coped with her husband's diagnosis for the benefit of others. For example, a hospital could invest in designing the most beautiful, state-of-the-art radiology or endoscopy room, but patients are often unconscious during such procedures and wouldn't benefit from the investment. Changing rooms, in contrast, were where patients and their families spent time talking and thinking about their situations, where they needed as much privacy, dignity, and comfort as possible. Blossfeld wanted to provide those things for people like her husband and herself.

That's why Blossfeld does what she does. Think about how to tell the story of why *you* do what you do, and how it might inspire and motivate others.

ORIENT AND MOTIVATE NEW EMPLOYEES

Kevin Weinstein is the chief growth officer of Valance Health, which delivers technology and platform-based solutions to healthcare facilities and providers. The corporate mission is to help healthcare providers modify their clinical and financial incentives so that they can focus on keeping people healthy, instead of treating them only when they are sick. Weinstein's tenure began in 2012, and the company grew from 250 employees to 950 by 2016, with a 450% increase in revenue. In this context, he recognized that new employees needed orientation not only to their roles and tasks, but to the growing organization's values and culture as well. So he tells a story that he heard years ago at an industry conference, one that really resonated with him.

At that conference, Dr. Brent James from Intermountain Healthcare System told his audience why healthcare must change. Intermountain Healthcare has hospitals across Utah. In the mid-to-late 1990s, the system had a protocol that required elaborate intervention for moderately premature newborns. First, the baby would be kept in an incubator to provide warmth and a consistent environment. Many would also be intubated, with a breathing tube placed down their throats to help with respiration. Second, the premature baby would be "packed up" and transported to the neonatal intensive care unit (NICU) in Salt Lake City, regardless of the hospital in which she was born. In many cases, this standard procedure meant the baby would be transported far from her parents, leaving them with a challenging, expensive commute or long wait for updates.

It's not hard to imagine how difficult it would be for parents, especially new mothers, who've just undergone the trauma of delivery, to deal with the stress of have their baby packed up and whisked hundreds of miles from them. I don't even have to imagine it, as I lived through a similar experience. In 2011, my younger daughter was delivered full-term by C-section, but the hospital told me that her low blood sugar level required transfer to the NICU. As I recovered from the surgery, my husband pushed my wheelchair back and forth between my recovery room and her NICU crib. I spent the first twenty-four hours after her birth watching nurses prick her tiny heels hourly for blood tests. Her heels were so bruised that they bled as soon as the bandages were removed. Later, when she was allowed to come home with us, our pediatrician frowned over the impossibly high blood sugar level the hospital required for newborns. The whole experience soured us to the facility and hospitals in general. Even five years later, my heart still aches over the memory. I was just a few floors from my daughter, so I can only imagine the pain of being separated by a much longer span of distance and time, as new parents in the Intermountain Healthcare System routinely were.

Luckily, as Dr. James told his conference audience, including Kevin Weinstein, someone came up with a simple but powerful idea: instead of following procedures that separated newborns from their mothers, the hospital outfitted mini intensive-care units within the mothers' recovery rooms. The new rooms included baby-appropriate versions of CPAP machines (like those used to treat sleep apnea in adults), which pump air into breathing passages. No incubation, no intubation, no transfer to a far-away NICU. What's more, this kinder, gentler intervention was just as effective as the much more stressful protocol. After a successful pilot program, the new practice was rolled out to the entire Intermountain Healthcare System. The downside was that the hospital system lost money because the new protocol involved fewer procedures and less staff time, and thus resulted in less billable service. In fact, the hospital lost over a million dollars a year because of the switch. But Intermountain still implemented the protocol because it was simply the right thing to do.

No good deed goes unpunished, right? Intermountain Healthcare ultimately ended up getting "punished" because it did the right thing by its patients. The US healthcare system generally still pays for procedures performed rather than higher-quality outcomes, though this is changing slowly under the Affordable Care Act at the time of this writing in September 2016. The longstanding reimbursement system has created disincentive for hospitals to innovate, in general, as illustrated by the Intermountain story.

Kevin Weinstein tells this story often to illustrate why healthcare needs to change. Sure, he could make the same point with complex facts, figures, and charts. But the simple story of newborns being packed up and sent away from their parents makes the argument much more effectively, with relate-ability and emotional punch. Valance Health aims to improve healthcare *outcome* quality, just as the Intermountain solution did, so the story illustrates well for new employees why Weinstein is excited to come to work every day, and why the new employees are part of an important, meaningful mission.

As you can see from Weinstein's example, you don't even need to come up with your own story. If you have come across stories that really speak to you, then use them (with permission, if needed) to inspire and motivate others. Motivating your employees in a complex industry is as much about leveraging the right emotional elements, such as those related to your organization's purpose and mission, as it is about using data-based arguments and financial incentives. Weinstein calls it "social reinforcement," or providing your team the right stories to reinforce their dedication to their work and goals.

SIMPLIFY A COMPLEX TOPIC

Stroke can happen at any age, according to the National Stroke Association, and is the fifth leading cause of death in the US.[3] Of those who survive strokes, more than two thirds suffer some disability. This is why identifying early symptoms and getting patients to hospitals well equipped to treat stroke are critical, says Faisal Khan, marketing manager at Stryker Neurovascular. One of the products in Khan's portfolio is a device physicians use to remove blood clots from patients suffering ischemic stroke, or an obstruction within a blood vessel.

Khan is also keenly aware that the way stroke is explained can be confusing and unintuitive, to say the least. For example, he learned about stroke through reading medical journals and attending physician-run seminars. In an email to me he described how a specific case of ischemic stroke and its treatment was explained to him.

It's important to identify the signs and symptoms of ischemic stroke early. It's equally important to ensure that the stroke patient is sent to a primary or comprehensive stroke center—doing so improves long-term patient outcomes.

For example, Mari, a 43-year-old female, had a wake-up stroke identified by her husband via symptoms of hemiparesis and aphasia (onset time unknown). From the local hospital, Mari was airlifted to a comprehensive stroke center, where she was diagnosed with an LVO. The interventional team decided to treat endovascularly, and deployed a mechanical thrombectomy device. The clot burden was removed in the first pass, leading to a TICI 3 acute outcome. Mari has gone on to mRS 0 at 90 days.

As you can see, these two paragraphs have a lot of information, but are littered with medical terms that can make understanding of stroke and its treatment difficult for most audiences. So Khan and his team developed short videos featuring real patients who'd survived ischemic strokes without long-term disability.[4]

In one of the videos, you meet Mari Dunsmore (the same Mari in the email above), a schoolteacher and mother of twin boys, as she and her husband Phil describe her stroke experience from her home in central California. They talk about how she woke up one night and felt something was wrong. The video also features Dr. Robert Taylor, Mari's attending physician, who describes how he retrieved the blood clot that caused the stroke using a device manufactured by Stryker.[5] It's clear that life for the Dunsmores would have been very different had Phil not made the decision to get Mari to a medical facility that night, rather than letting her go back to bed, as she wished. The short but highly effective video communicates just enough information and emotion to alert viewers to watch for signs of stroke, including difficulty speaking and numbness in the face, arm, or leg.[6]

MAKE HEALTHCARE DATA PERSONAL

Ashish V. Shah has a knack for humanizing data. He's the co-founder of PreparedHealth, a healthcare social network that optimizes clinical quality and finance by connecting healthcare providers, health plans, patients, and their families. One client of PreparedHealth is a large, privately owned home-healthcare company that covers everything from in-home nursing to hospice services. Not unlike most large healthcare organizations, each service line was operated as an independent business unit. Shah and his team were convinced that the client was missing a large untapped opportunity to integrate various business-unit service offerings, which would result in better holistic care and overall patient loyalty. So they dug into the data to find out.

Once Shah had an integration strategy in mind, based on the data, he met with the client's executive board. But he didn't present any data at first. Instead, he told the story of two seventy-something clients who lived in the same retirement community. In great detail, he described each individual's healthcare journey over time, including the many services of the client they benefited from, while also showing how disconnected these were, requiring trips to multiple facilities and visits to many different providers. At the end of the story, he revealed that the two were actually husband and wife, married for quite some time. They were not two separate patients, but rather a family that could have really benefited from a holistic care management experience. The story helped the board understand just how disjointed their services were, and inspired them to work toward better integration.

With vivid images from Shah's story in mind, executives were able to take fast, practical steps to enhance the healthcare experience for their customers. Not only were Shah's audience members inspired to act, but they were able to repeat the story to their colleagues and partner organizations, amplifying its power. The outcome highlights the effectiveness of distilling conclusions based on a large set of data into simple but compelling human stories.

CRAFT AN EFFECTIVE LEADERSHIP STORY

In 2015, Neha Agrawal (not her real name), a marketing executive at a global medical device company, was selected as one of the opening speakers at her company's multi-day leadership off-site. In front of peer senior executives, her charge was to set the tone for the day and speak on the topic of leadership. She had about forty-five minutes to speak, with no other specific guidelines.

What would you talk about in Agrawal's position? Maybe you'd talk about the latest academic research on leadership and how the company's senior team can implement the new insights. Or the state of leadership at her company and how it can be challenged and elevated.

Agrawal decided against such possibilities. Instead, she told her audience of managers the story of climbing Mount Kilimanjaro in 2008 with her parents, sister, husband, and three children—nine people representing three generations and ranging in age from seven to seventy. Not a single one was an outdoor-adventurer type. "We're more like eaters and strollers," Uppal said.

So Agrawal did everything she could to prepare everyone for the trip. For example, she guided the packing of everything each person needed each night in a separate Ziploc bag with a clear label, to avoid confusion on the mountain. Of course, they still faced plenty of obstacles, including challenges posed by her seventy-year-old parents' health, and that children weren't allowed past the second climbing station.

For forty-five minutes, Agrawal regaled her audiences with the riveting tale of this extraordinary family journey, with humility and humor. Given the event's theme, she ended with a list of leadership lessons:

- Allow yourself to be inspired.
- Prepare your team well.
- Admit it is scary and hard, and allow your team to lift you up.
- Recognize all the different forms of leadership you will need.
- Realize that some things and people will need to stop before the final destination.
- Break it down into small steps.
- Use your resources strategically.
- Pass leadership lessons forward.

Agrawal's choice to tell her family's travel story might be unconventional. But she could tell that the audience was fully engaged, and many listeners shared their own family adventures and lessons learned with her afterward.

This is one of the best indicators that your story is effective: when it inspires others to share their own. The best stories resonate and lead to more stories, allowing us to connect deeply with others through this vital form of communication.

EPILOGUE

I STARTED THIS BOOK WITH an epiphany from my days as an admissions officer. Let me end the book with another admissions story.

Mark (not his real name) applied to six top-tier business schools in 2013 on his own and got rejected by all of them. A year later, I had the opportunity to advise him as he reapplied. Of the four top-ten American business schools he applied to on his second try, he was accepted by all four! Not only did he go from 0 to 100%, he was offered major scholarships by two of the schools.

But this is not where Mark's story ended.

After he accepted his spot at Wharton, he realized that the competition had barely started. Once at an elite business school where everyone was a rock star, he had to compete to get on companies' interview schedules. He had to compete in business case competitions. He even had to compete to get into popular classes. One such class required an extensive application process, and the school told students: "If you're a first-year student, don't bother."

Well, Mark wanted to get in as a first-year student, so he applied anyway . . . and he got in! Later on, he was told that his essay, a well-told story about why he deserved a spot, tipped the decision.

Life is a perpetual competitive admissions game. I hope you have gotten plenty of ideas from this book on how to tell your stories. It requires time and dedication to own the tools and concepts. But I know it will pay off for you!

I'd love to hear how you apply what you have learned from this book. Please connect with me:

Esther@LeadershipStorylab.com
LinkedIn.com/EstherChoy
Twitter: @LeaderStoryLab

NOTES

INTRODUCTION

1   There is growing evidence for the neurobiological basis for the power of storytelling to make us remember and act. See for example Paul Zak, "Why Your Brain Loves Good Storytelling," *Harvard Business Review*, October 28, 2014, https://hbr.org/2014/10/why-your-brain-loves-good-storytelling/ (accessed April 13, 2015).

2   Robert McKee, *Story: Substance, Structure, Style, and the Principles of Screenwriting*, HarperCollins Publishers, New York, p. 28.

3   Robert Cialdini, *Influence: The Psychology of Persuasion*, Harper Business, New York, 2006.

CHAPTER 1

1   This story is based on the experience of an acquaintance, with key details disguised.

2   Chip and Dan Heath, *Switch*, Crown Business, 2010. Note that the Heaths use an excellent analogy, comparing rationality to a rider and emotion to an elephant in regard to decision-making. To make optimal decisions, you have to engage both rider and elephant effectively, rationality and emotion.

3   Radio Lab, "Overcome by Emotion" NPR podcast, http://www.radiolab.org/story/91642-overcome-by-emotion/

4   Allan Weiss, *Million Dollar Consulting*, McGraw Hill Education, 5th Edition, April 2016

5   Matthew Weiner, "Wait Wait... Don't Tell Me!" Chicago Public Radio, Chicago, March 2015. http://www.npr.org/2015/03/28/395741081/not-my-job-mad-men-creator-matthew-weiner-gets-quizzed-on-glad-men (accessed June 28, 2016).

6   Alex Baydin, "What I Learned When My Company Almost Went Bankrupt," *Fortune*, May 24, 2016, http://fortune.com/author/alex-baydin/ (accessed June 28, 2016).

7   Kathleen Doheny, "Autism Cases on the Rise; Reason for Increase a Mystery," WebMD, March 28 2008. http://www.webmd.com/brain/autism/searching-for-answers/autism-rise (accessed June 29, 2016).

8   Adam Mordecai, "16 years ago, a doctor published a study. It was completely made up, and it made us all sicker," *Upworthy*, December 5, 2014.
http://www.upworthy.com/16-years-ago-a-doctor-published-a-study-it-was-completely-made-up-and-it-made-us-all-sicker?c=ufb7 (accessed June 29, 2016).

9   Clifford Krauss, "Oil Prices: What's Behind the Drop? Simple Economics," *New York Times*, January 6, 2016.
http://www.nytimes.com/interactive/2016/business/energy-environment/oil-prices.html?_r=0 (accessed June 29, 2016).

CHAPTER 2

1   Paul Dolan, *Happiness by Design*, Plume Publishing, 2014, p. 150.

2   This chapter is inspired by the book *The Seven Basic Plots* by Christopher Booker. Continuum, 2004.

3   Kurt Vonnegut, *A Man Without A Country*, Random House, 2005, pp. 23-31.

4   Google "Vonnegut shape of story" to find additional reading and even a YouTube video of the author himself describing his story graphs in detail.

5   Richard Feloni, "Pepsi CEO Indra Nooyi explains how an unusual daily ritual her mom made her practice as a child changed her life." Business Insider, September 5, 2015. http://www.businessinsider.com/pepsico-indra-nooyi-life-changing-habit-2015-9 (June 29, 2016).

6   Kathleen Elkins, "From poverty to a $3 billion fortune —the incredible rags-to-riches story of Oprah Winfrey." *Business Insider*, May 28, 2015, http://www.businessinsider.com/rags-to-riches-story-of-oprah-winfrey-2015-5 (accessed June 29, 2016).

7   Dennis Romero, "Homelessness, Hair Care and 12,000 Bottles of Tequila," *Entrepreneur*, June 11, 2009. https://www.entrepreneur.com/article/202258 (accessed June 29, 2016).

8   Christopher Booker, *The Seven Basic Plots*, Continuum, 2004, p. 194.

9   Richard Teerlink, AMA Motorcycle Hall of Fame, Inducted in 2015. http://www.motorcyclemuseum.org/halloffame/detail.aspx?RacerID=475 (accessed June 29, 2016).

10 Scott Bieber, "Harley Is 'A Classic Turnaround Story' Executive Interview Vaughn Beals, Harley-davidson Inc." *The Morning Call.* April 18, 1988. (accessed June 29, 2016)
http://articles.mcall.com/1988-04-18/business/2634587_1_harley-dealers-american-motorcycle-manufacturer-big-motorcycles (accessed June 29, 2016)

11 Richard Teerlink, AMA Motorcycle Hall of Fame, Inducted in 2015. http://www.motorcyclemuseum.org/halloffame/detail.aspx?RacerID=475 (accessed June 29, 2016)

12   Glenn Rifkin, "How Harley Davidson Revs Its Brand" *iStrategy + Business*, Oct 1, 1997. http://www.strategy-business.com/article/12878?gko=ffaa3 (accessed June 29, 2016)

13   Lisa Stein, "Living with Cancer: Kris Carr's Story." ScientificAmerican.com, July 16, 2008. http://www.scientificamerican.com/article/living-with-cancer-kris-carr/ (accessed June 29, 2016).

14   Pure Earth and Green Cross, "World's Worst Pollution Problems 2015" Pure Earth and Green Cross, Zurich Switzerland, 2015. http://www.worstpolluted.org (accessed June 29, 2016).

15   Raveena Aulakh, "10 toxic pollution success stories" TheStar.com, Jan 27, 2015. https://www.thestar.com/news/world/2015/01/27/10-toxic-pollution-success-stories.html (accessed June 29, 2016).

16   Kitt Stapp, "Developing Nations Write Hopeful New Chapters in a Toxic Legacy" Inter Press Service, Jan 27 2015. http://www.ipsnews.net/2015/01/developing-nations-write-hopeful-new-chapters-in-a-toxic-legacy/ (accessed June 29, 2016).

17   Alex Kotlowitz, "The Thin Blue Ribbon." Chicago Public Radio, June 15 2016. http://www.heatofthemoment.org/features/astronaut/ (accessed June 29, 2016).

18   http://www.dyson.com/community/aboutdyson.aspx (accessed June 29, 2016).

19   Stephen Dubnar, "How to create suspense." Freakonomics.com July 29, 2015. http://freakonomics.com/podcast/how-to-create-suspense-a-new-freakonomics-radio-episode/ (accessed June 30, 2016).

20   If you are a procrastinator (like me!) and do not have that luxury of putting it aside for a day, then at least leave your draft alone for an hour or two and do something completely different.

21   See previous footnote.

22   Robert McKee, *Story* HarperCollins, 1997, p. 76.

23   This example is based on the following article: http://www.telegraph.co.uk/technology/news/9525267/Airbnb-The-story-behind-the-1.3bn-room-letting-website.html (accessed June 30, 2016).

24   The example is based on this article: "Homelessness, Hair Care and 12,000 Bottles of Tequila," *Entrepreneur* https://www.entrepreneur.com/article/202258 (accessed June 30, 2016).

25   Example based on these articles: "Sallie Krawcheck Remembers Her Twenties Being 'A Lost Journey' —Until One Amazing Day Changed Everything" from *Business Insider*; "I Knew I Would Get Fired," from *Fast Company*; and "Sallie Krawcheck: From Wall Street Boss to Entrepreneur," Radiate Podcast.

26   Example based on this article: http://www.scientificamerican.com/article/living-with-cancer-kris-carr/ (accessed July 1, 2016).

27   Adapted from Adair Lara's book *Naked, Drunk, and Writing* (Ten Speed Press, 2010).

CHAPTER 3

1   Jon Scieszka, *The True Story of the 3 Little Pigs!*, Puffin Books, 1989.

2   I did not work as a consultant for either party in the U.S. Bank acquisition. I created this example based on public information. All quotes are inspired by or paraphrased based on reporting by journalists at the *Chicago Tribune, USA Today*, and ShelterForce.com, as cited in subsequent text. However, for full disclosure, I was a former Charter One Bank customer!

3   (accessed August 18, 2016).

4   (accessed August 18, 2016).

5   (accessed August 18, 2016).

6   (accessed August 18, 2016).

7   ibid.

8   Based on information about banks and low-income neighborhoods from: Peter Skillern, "When Your Bank Leaves Town: How Communities Can Fight Back," Shelterforce Online, 126 (2002): http://www.shelterforce. com/online/issues/126/bankclosings.html (accessed August 18, 2016).

CHAPTER 4

1   Kim Nash, "ADP's CIO Says Algorithms Measure Employee Flight Risk" *Wall Street Journal*, May 31, 2016. http://blogs.wsj.com/cio/2016/05/31/ adp-algorithms-tackle-employee-flight-risk/ (accessed June 14, 2016)

2   Hiawatha Bray, "When the Billboard Has A Brain," *The Boston Globe*, May 19, 2016 https://www.bostonglobe.com/business/2016/05/18/when-billboard-has-brain/TjUFP907S0nUKmqsLihsaN/story.html (accessed June 14, 2016)

3   Meta Brown, "Big Data Analytics and the Next President: How Microtargeting Drives Today's Campaigns" Forbes.com May 29, 2016 http://www.forbes.com/sites/metabrown/2016/05/29/big-data-analytics-and-the-next-president-how-microtargeting-drives-todays-campaigns/#27ed07371400 (accessed June 14, 2016)

4   Data-related categories as defined by Gartner, www.gartner.com/it-glossary/big-data (accessed June 14, 2016)

5   Amy Affelt, "Acting on Big Data: A Data Scientist Role for Info Pros," RsearchGate.com, September 2014. https://www.researchgate.net/publication/269698040_Acting_on_Big_Data_A_Data_Scientist_Role_for_Info_Pros (accessed June 14, 2016)

6   Jim Stikeleather, "How to Tell a Story with Data" *Harvard Business Review* Blog, April 24, 2013. https://hbr.org/2013/04/how-to-tell-a-story-with-data/ (accessed June 14, 2016); descriptions of audience types reflect my additions and modifications.

7   Jim Stikeleather, "How to Tell a Story with Data" *Harvard Business Review* Blog, April 24, 2013. https://hbr.org/2013/04/how-to-tell-a-story-with-data/ (accessed June 14, 2016)

8   Nicolas Malo, "5 questions on Data Storytelling to Brent Dykes, Evangelist for Customer Analytics at Adobe" http://www.nicolasmalo.com/web_analytics_ecommerce_e/2015/06/5-questions-on-data-storytelling-to-brent-dykes-evangelist-for-customer-analytics-at-adobe.html (accessed June 14, 2016)

9   Jag Bhalla, "It Is in Our Nature to Need Stories," *Scientific American*, May 8, 2013, http://blogs.scientificamerican.com/guest-blog/it-is-in-our-nature-to-need-stories/ (accessed June 14, 2016).

10   George Miller, paper "The Magical Number Seven, Plus or Minus Two," *Psychological Review*, Vol. 101, No. 2, 343-352, May 1955.

11   Nour Kteily, Gordon Hudson, and Emile Bruneau, *Journal of Personality and Social Psychology*, "They See Us As Less Than Human: Meta-Dehumanization Predicts Intergroup Conflict Via Reciprocal Dehumanization" December 2015 https://www.researchgate.net/publication/286780003 (accessed June 15, 2016)

12   Emily Stone, "How Hateful Rhetoric Can Create a Vicious Cycle of Dehumanization" *Kellogg Insight*, Jan 2016. http://insight.kellogg.northwestern.edu/article/how-hateful-rhetoric-can-create-a-vicious-cycle-of-dehumanization/ (accessed June 15, 2016)

13   Susan Etlinger, "What Do We Do with All This Big Data?" TED September 2014, https://www.ted.com/talks/susan_etlinger_what_do_we_do_with_all_this_big_data/transcript?language=en#t-525270 (accessed June 15, 2016)

14   Simon Sinek, *Start with Why*, Portfolio, 2011.

15   Nicolas Malo, "5 Questions on Data Storytelling to Brent Dykes, Evangelist for Customer Analytics at Adobe" NicolasMalo.com http://www.nicolasmalo.com/web_analytics_ecommerce_e/2015/06/5-questions-on-data-storytelling-to-brent-dykes-evangelist-for-customer-analytics-at-adobe.html (accessed June 17, 2016)

16   US Department of Transportation, "Jason's Law Truck Parking Survey Results and Comparative Analysis" August 2015. http://www.ops.fhwa.dot.gov/freight/infrastructure/truck_parking/jasons_law/truckparkingsurvey/jasons_law.pdf (accessed June 17, 2016).

17   Lynn Thompson, "As big rigs overwhelm parking, nervous North Bend looks at limits" *Seattle Times*, March 29, 2016. http://www.seattletimes.com/seattle-news/eastside/as-big-rigs-overwhelm-parking-nervous-north-bend-looks-at-limits/ (accessed June 17, 2016).

18   Aarian Marshall, "Parking a Truck Is a Pain in the Butt. Tech to the Rescue!" *Wired*, June 6 2016 https://www.wired.com/2016/06/parking-truck-pain-butt-tech-rescue (accessed June 17, 2016).

CHAPTER 5

1   For my non-finance readers, an asset class is anything you can invest in. Among the more common ones are stocks, bonds, and precious metals like gold. More complex asset class such as collateralized debt obligations are newer and tend to be riskier.

2   Larry Jacoby, "Becoming Famous Overnight: Limits on the Ability to Avoid Unconscious Influences of the Past." *Journal of Personality and Social Psychology*, 1989, Vol. 56, No. 3, 326 – 328. Daniel Kahneman, Thinking Fast and Slow, p. 61.

3   http://www.nytimes.com/2016/09/15/technology/personaltech/iphone-7-review-though-not-perfect-new-iphones-keep-apples-promises.html?smprod=nytcore-iphone&smid=nytcore-iphone-share

4   Charles Wheelan, *Naked Statistics*, W. W. Norton & Company, 2014.

5   David Brooks, "Poetry of Everyday Life," *New York Times*, April 11, 2011.

CHAPTER 6

1   Eric Kandell, James Schwartz, Thomas Jessell, Steven Siegelbaum, A.J. Hudspeth, *Principles of Neural Science*, 5th Edition, McGraw-Hill Education / Medical; 5th edition, October 2012.

2   Freakonomics Radio, Should US Merge with Mexico? November 6, 2014 http://freakonomics.com/podcast/should-the-u-s-merge-with-mexico-a-new-freakonomics-radio-podcast/

CHAPTER 7

1   Malcolm Gladwell talks about the "Rule of 10,000 Hours," describing how it takes about that much practice and learning to master a given skill. Though others have disputed this claim, the general concept that mastery requires extensive, varied practice is sound. See *Outliers: The Story of Success*, Little, Brown, and Company, 2008.

2   http://www.npr.org/templates/story/story.php?storyId=128239303 (accessed July 19, 2016).

3   Doug Lipman, "Improving Your Storytelling: Beyond the Basics for All Who Tell Stories in Work and Play," August House, 1999, p. 18.

4   Tony Schwartz, "The Only Thing That Matters," *Harvard Business Review* blog, June 2011. https://hbr.org/2011/06/the-only-thing-that-really-mat.html (accessed July 19, 2016).

5   Peter Kadens, keynote speaker at the Executive Studio Network April 28 2016 meeting in Chicago.

6   http://time.com/3858309/attention-spans-goldfish/ (accessed July 20, 2016).

7   Annette Simmons, "Whoever Tells the Best Story Wins," AMACOM BOOKS, 2007, p. 206.

8   I first saw this brilliant quote as a LinkedIN repost from a former classmate. Unfortunately, the source is unknown. If you do, please contact me! Esther@LeadershipStoryLab.com

9   R. B. van Baaren, R. W. Holland, B Steenaert and A. Knippenberg. "Mimicry for Money: Behavioral Consequences of Imitation," *Journal of Experimental Social Psychology*, 39: 393–98.

CHAPTER 8

1   Robert Cialdini, Influence: *The Psychology of Persuasion*, Harper Business, New York, 2006.

2   Lauren Rivera, "Hirable Like Me," Northwestern University, April 3 2013. http://insight.kellogg.northwestern.edu/article/hirable_like_me and, Lauren Rivera, "Hiring as Cultural Matching", Association of Sociological Review, 77(6) 999-1022, http://www.asanet.org/journals/ASR/Dec12ASRFeature.pdf

3   For more on the reasons that finding common ground boosts your chances of interview success, see Lauren Rivera, "Go with Your Gut: Emotion and Evaluation in Job Interviews," *American Journal of Sociology*, Vol. 120, No. 5, March 2015, pp. 1339-1389.

4   *Freakonomics Radio Live* in St. Paul, October 11, 2011, http://www.youtube.com/watch?v=g495pyl2G1Y&list=PL5E9D4FB04FB17DB2

5   *Worth Repeating: More Than 5,000 Classic and Contemporary Quotes* (2003) by Bob Kelly, p. 263.

CHAPTER 9

1   For more on introverts and networking see Marty Nemko, "Networking for People That Dislike It," *Psychology Today*, March 20, 2015, https://www.psychologytoday.com/blog/how-do-life/201503/networking-people-dislike-it (accessed April 7, 2015).

2   As discussed in Susan Adams, "Why You Hate Networking," *Forbes*, September 16, 2014, http://www.forbes.com/sites/susanadams/2014/09/16/why-you-hate-networking/ (accessed April 7, 2015).

3   Andrew Stanton, "The Clues to a Great Story," TED Talk, February 2012, http://www.ted.com/talks/andrew_stanton_the_clues_to_a_great_story?language=en (accessed April 7, 2015).

4   Graham Gibbs, "Twenty Terrible Reasons for Lecturing," SCED Occasional Paper No. 8, Birmingham, 1981.

CHAPTER 10

1   Penelope Burk, "Where Philanthropy Is Headed," by The Burk Donor Survey, August 2016 http://cygresearch.com/dev/?page_id=14170

2   Eric Ries, *The Lean Startup*, Crown Business, September 2011.

3   Kevin Systrom, "How I Built It," National Public Radio podcast hosted by Guy Raz, September 2016 https://www.statista.com/statistics/253577/number-of-monthly-active-instagram-users/

4   Karen Jenni & George Lowenstein, "Explaining the Identifiable Victim Effect," *Journal of Risk and Uncertainty*, p. 236, 1997.

5   Compiled from FOS and similar organizations. https://www.floridaocean.org/p/3/about-us#.V7h5mGU9VFI; http://www.teamorca.org/cfiles/orcawishlist.cfm

https://www.floridaocean.org/uploads/docs/blocks/222/2016-coastal-disc-registration-packet.pdf
http://www.pacificmmc.org/sponsor-a-classroom/#sthash.eRUyDOR8.dpuf
https://www.floridaocean.org/p/245/annual-report#.V7iAjWU9VFI
http://www.conserveturtles.org/support.php?page=funding_ideas
http://chesapeakebay.noaa.gov/fish-facts/oysters

6   http://oneruntogether.org/about-us/
Compiled from OneRunTogether and related sources
http://www.restockit.com/food-and-breakroom-supplies/water-and-beverages/bottled-water.html
http://www.timingconsortium.com/pricing.htm
http://www.timingconsortium.com/pricing.htm
https://www.weaversorchard.com/festivals-events/5k-mud-run/
http://www.uberprints.com/make/5k-race-shirts

7   Compiled from SOS Children Villages Illinois and related sources
https://www.sosillinois.org
https://www.sosillinois.org/about-us/
https://www.sosillinois.org/about-us/
https://www.sosillinois.org/2nd-annual-back-to-school-supply-drive/
https://www.sosillinois.org/youth-mental-health-understanding-engaging-destigmatizing/
https://www.sosillinois.org/make-it-better-foundation-makes-a-difference-at-sos-illinois/
https://www.sosillinois.org/family-fun-at-the-circus/
https://www.sosillinois.org/youth-mental-health-understanding-engaging-destigmatizing/
https://www.sosillinois.org/summer-adventures-at-summer-camp/
https://www.sosillinois.org/summer-adventures-at-summer-camp/

CHAPTER 11

1   http://www.narrativemedicine.org/mission.html

2   http://www.fiercehealthcare.com/healthcare/mass-general-s-sharingclinic-bets-big-healthcare-storytelling

3   www.stroke.org.

4   I encourage you to watch the videos not only as examples of effective storytelling in healthcare but also to learn how to watch for stroke symptoms in yourself or others. See https://www.youtube.com/watch?v=JANFZrpt1Hg

5   Dr. Taylor used a device called Trevo, manufactured and distributed by Stryker Neurovascular.

6   For more information on symptoms of stroke, visit the Mayo Clinic website: http://www.mayoclinic.org/diseases-conditions/stroke/symptoms-causes/dxc-20117265

INDEX

Acknowledge–Inspire–Action (AIA) model, 53–55, 63, 81–82, 90, 95–96
acknowledging others, 134–136
action, generating, 11, 69–70
Adobe, 73, 85
Advertising Research Foundation, 67
Affordable Care Act, 207
aggressive listening, 140–147
Airbnb, 36–37
Aitken, Jason, 95–96
Alger, Horatio, 27
Al-Jazeera News, 21
Altimeter Group, 80
Angelou, Maya, on how you make people feel, 9
Apple, 93–94
Arntson, Paul, on listening, 141
AT&T, 65
attention spans, 141
audience(s), 47–64
    acknowledging your, 54
    and AIA model, 53–55
    caring for your, 51–53
    data and categories of, 70–73
    external factors with, 10–11
    "fit" of story with, 34
    as focus of the story, 18–19
    inspiration for entrepreneur vs. for, 49–50
    internal factors with, 9–10
    knowing your, 8–11
    "Look Who's Listening" approach to, 55–64
    starting with point of view of the, 189–190
    and telling your story, 154
    and Three Little Pigs story, 47–49
authenticity, 6
autism, 19–20

Baydin, Alex, on fear of missing payroll, 15–16
belief, 123–124
Bible, 30
Bieber, Scott, on Harley-Davidson motorbikes, 29
Big Data, 65–66, 80, 82
binding agents, 119
Bladt, Jeff, on data scientists, 73–74
Blossfeld, Maureen, 204–205
body, listening with your, 143–144
Booker, Christopher, 29
Booth School of Business, xv
boss, as audience, 72
Brexit, 18
Brooks, David, on metaphors, 94
Bruneau, Emile, 79
Bubble Academy, 50
Budweiser, 30
business school applicants, communicating with rejected, xv–xvii, 213

career ladder, moving up the, 21–22
career matrix, 181–184
caring for your audience, 51–53, 204
Carlisle, Danny, 163–164

Carr, Kris, 30, 41
categorizing, when networking, 175
Central Limit Theorem, 94
challenge (as story element), 12, 15
change
    resistance to, 54
    in storytelling, 15, 34–35
    using graphs to display, 109–110
Charter One Bank, 56–64
China, 7–8
Choy, Esther, 42–43
Cialdini, Robert, *xxi*, 152
clarifying questions, asking, 145
Clear Channel Outdoor, 65
client needs, recognizing, 140
Clinton–Trump election, 18
Closed End, 17
Coben, Harlan, on hope, 33
colleagues, cross-functional, 71
colleagues, getting to know, 139–140
collecting stories, 129–147
    and acknowledgment of others,
        134–136
    and aggressive listening, 140–147
    and asking "crazy good"
        questions, 136–139
    and client needs, 140
    and getting to know colleagues,
        139–140
    and point of view, 130–133
    and practice as storyteller, 130
communication, of data analytics, 69
communication mastery, three stages
    of, 21–22
communicators, master, 22
"competitive admissions" game,
    xviii–xx
complex, explaining the, 89–97
    by comparing unfamiliar to
        familiar, 92–94
    by dividing and conquering,
        90–92
    in healthcare industry case study,
        208–209
    by using a happy ending, 96–97
    by utilizing a strong structure,
        95–96
conflict (as story element), 13–14

Congress, 32
contradiction (as story element),
    13–15
contrast (as story element), 13–14
conversational hooks, in networking,
    175–176
Council of Economic Advisers (CEA),
    110–111
"crazy good" questions, asking,
    136–139
cross-functional colleagues, as
    audience, 71
"Curse of Knowledge," 67–68, 74
customers, "Looks Who's Listening"
    approach with, 56–64

data, 65–88
    advantages of storytelling over,
        73–74
    example of structuring story
        around, 85–88
    and five audience categories,
        70–73
    overabundance of, 66–67
    personalizing of, in healthcare
        industry case study, 209–
        210
    process for weaving story and,
        74–85
    and storytelling, 67–70
data analytics, 68
decision-making
    and emotion, 7, 9
    using data to support, 70–71
DeJoria, John Paul, 28, 38
Democratic Republic of the Congo,
    117
"dividing and conquering," with
    complex topics, 90–92
Dolan, Paul, on calculation of time, 24
Dubner, Stephen J., 110–111, 158,
    160–161
Dunsmore, Mari, 209
Dykes, Brent, on data storytelling,
    73, 85
Dyson, James, 32

Eat, Pray, Love (Elizabeth Gilbert), 23

Einstein, Albert, on logic vs. imagination, 174
elements of a story, 6
emotion, 7–8
    and decision making, 7, 9
    "right" level of, 32–33
empathy
    in data-based presentations, 74–76
    and listening, 144–145
employees, motivating new, 205–208
entrepreneur, inspiration for, vs. for the audience, 49–50
Etlinger, Susan, on creating meaning, 80
European Union, 18
extracurricular activities, 21

fact-based stories, 20–21
familiar, comparing unfamiliar to, 92–94
FEE (Freestyling for Everything Else), 114–117
feedback
    asking for, 165, 169
    getting, on StoryPictures, 124
    for rejected business school applicants, xv
fellow experts, as audience, 72
Filbin, Bob, on data scientists, 73–74
"film director," being a, 142–143
filtering, 34
Finding Nemo (film), 176
"first draft, ugly," 33
"fit," xvii, 34
Five Basic Plots, 24
follow-up questions, 10
Forbes, 65
Ford, Harrison, 31
formulas, 112–113
Fortune, 15
Fox, Vicente, 110
Franconeri, Steve, on impact of visual elements, 99
Freakonomics (Harlan Coben and Stephen Dubner), 33, 110, 160
Freakonomics Radio, 158

George VI, King, 29–30
Gibbs, Graham, on ineffectiveness of lecturing, 176
Global Financial Crisis, 53
Goolsbee, Austan, 110–111
governing principles, 112
graphs, 109–110
Greenpeace Switzerland, 30
gut, going with your, 7

happy endings, with complex topics, 96–97
Harley-Davidson, 29
Harvard Business Review, 71, 74, 134
"Head Cheese," as audience, 72, 73
healthcare industry (case study), 203–212
    and caring vs. knowing, 204
    and crafting an effective leadership story, 210–212
    and explaining what you do, 204–205
    handling complex topics in, 208–209
    and making data personal, 209–210
    motivating new employees in, 205–208
Heath brothers, 7
hedge funds, 51
Heitner, Michael, on preparing for presentations, 67
Hick, Andy, 156
Holister, Glenn, 53–55
hook(s), 13–15
    in Act I, 12
    conversational, in networking, 175–176
    when telling stories with data, 81
    when telling your own story, 155, 162, 164
hope, offering, 32–33
The Hot Club of San Francisco (Pandora station), 107
HSBC, 30
Hudson, Gordon, 79

Idea Quotient, 113

Identifiable Beneficiary Effect, 191
Identifiable Victim Effect, 191
imagination, 6
Indian Jones movies, 31
influencing others, 11
information, providing, in data-based
    presentations, 82–85
informing, 18
inspiration, for speaker vs. for the
    audience, 49–50
Instagram, 189
intelligent outsiders, as audience, 71,
    73
inter-group perceptions, 79
Intermountain Healthcare, 206–207
interrupting, with your own story, 145
interviewers, rankings by, 153
"intrigue and delight," 18
investment pitches, 51–53
iPhone, 93–94
Iran, 20

Jacoby, Larry, 93
James, Brent, 206–207
Jesus Christ, 28
joint ventures, 95–96

Kadens, Pete, "Mad Prop" program
    of, 136
Kahneman, Daniel, 93
Kansal, Reena, 16–17
Kansas City Royals, 132–133
Kellogg School of Management,
    151–153
Khan, Faisal, on treating stroke, 208
Kim, Greg, on data scientists, 66–67
King, Stephen, on being a writer, 130
The King's Speech (film), 30
Klees-Johnson, Gregoire, 49
Klees-Johnson, Kristine, 49
knowledge
    caring vs., 204
    conveying, 10
Krawcheck, Sallie, 39–40
Kteily, Nour, 79

The Lancet, 19
leadership, and persuasion, xviii

lecturing, 176
Levitt, Steven D., 158
likeability, 152–153, 160
"liking," as major lever of persuasion,
    xxi
Lipman, Doug, storytelling model of,
    131
listening, aggressive, 140–147
Liu, Di Fan, 7–8
"Look Who's Listening" approach,
    55–64

Mad Men (TV series), 15
"Mad Prop" program, 136
"The Magical Number Seven, Plus or
    Minus Two" (George Miller),
    78
Making of a Murderer (Netflix series),
    23
A Man Without a Country (Kurt
    Vonnegut), 24–26
Marshall, Aarian, 87
Massachusetts General Hospital, 204
master communicators, 22
McKee, Robert, xx, 34
meaning, creating, in data-based
    presentations, 80–82
metaphors, 94
Mexico, 30, 110
Michelin ratings, 52
Microsoft, 141
Miller, George, 78
Million Dollar Consulting (Alan
    Weiss), 7
mindset, 123–124
mini-admissions applications, xix–xx
monster, overcoming the, see
    overcoming the monster
Moore, Joel, on "dividing and
    conquering" in the financial
    industry, 91–92
Moses, 30
motivation, 6
Motorcylce Hall of Fame, 29
Murphy, Brian, on listening, 141

Naked Statistics (Charles Wheelan),
    94

narrative(s), 19–20, 73
NASA, 31–32
National Public Radio, 130
National Stroke Association, 208
Nature, 77
nested circles, 104–109
Netflix, 23
networking, 171–185
    and best resopnse to "What Do
        You Do?," 180–181
    and career matrix, 181–184
    dislike of, 172–174
    framework for effective, 174–177
    pattern of interaction in, 174–175
    and pre-crafting the
        conversation, 176–177, 181
    storytelling approach to, 177–180
    using conversational hooks in,
        175–176
New England Journal of Medicine, 77
New Oxford American Dictionary, 94
New York Mets, 133
New York Times, 32, 94
nonprofit organization storytelling,
    187–201
    and focusing on clear, direct
        results, 191–192
    Social Impact Story Outline in,
        192–201
    and starting with audience's point
        of view, 189–190
    and using the Identifiable
        Beneficiary Effect, 191
non-technical audiences, 68–69
Nooyi, Indra, 26–27
Northwestern University, 99, 141,
    151–153
numbers, words, vs., in data-based
    presentations, 78–80

Obama, Barack, 110
oil prices, 20–21
Open End, 16–17
origin story(-ies), 26–27
    change in, 35
    emotional impact of, 32
    example of, 36–37
    outline for, 36

outsiders, intelligent, as audience,
    71
overcoming the monster, 29–31
    change in, 35
    emotional impact of, 32
    example of, 41
    outline for, 40
Oxford Learning Institute, 176
Oxford University, 176

Pandora, 107
paraphrasing, 145
Pátron Spirits Company, 28
patterns, showing, 109
Paul Mitchell hair care system, 28
PepsiCo, 26–27
perceptions, inter-group, 79
PerformLine, 15
persuasion
    and communication, *xxi*
    with data, 69–70
    in data-based presentations, 77
    and leadership, *xviii*
    proof vs., 18
    and telling your story, 161–164
Philippines, 30
"physics envy," 112
pie charts, 110–111
pleasantries, exchanging, 174–175
plot(s), 23–43
    combining multiple types of, 33
    definition of, 23–24
    examples of five basic, 35–43
    learning to construct, 33–35
    origin as, 26–27
    overcoming the monster as, 29–31
    quest as, 31–32
    rags to riches as, 27–28
    rebirth as, 28–29
    and "right" emotional impact,
        32–33
    visual representations of, 25, 28
"Poetry of Everyday Life" (David
    Brooks), 94
points of view, 130–133
pollution, 30–31
poster-paper, 126
practicing, 130, 168–169

pre-crafting the conversation, when networking, 176–177, 181
PreparedHealth, 209–210
presentations, preparing for, 67
proving, persuading vs., 18
Pure Earth, 30

qualifications, value of a story vs. explaining your, *xvii–xviii*
questions
    asking "crazy good," 136–139
    from audience, 10
    clarifying, 145
quest story(-ies), 31–32
    change in, 35
    emotional impact of, 32
    example of, 42–43
    outline for, 42

rags to riches story(-ies), 27–28
    change in, 35
    emotional impact of, 32
    example of, 38
    outline for, 37–38
rebirth stories (-ies), 28–29
    change in, 35
    emotional impact of, 32
    example of, 39–40
    outline for, 39
redemption, stories of, 29
relationships, showing
    with FEE, 114–117
    with formulas, 112–113
    with graphs, 109–110
    with pie charts, 110–111
    with Venn diagrams, 104–109
Republic of the Congo, 115–117
results, focusing on clear and direct, 191–192
Revolutionary War, 133
Ries, Eric, on asking users why they use apps, 189
risk scores, 92–93
Rivera, Lauren, on rankings by interviewers, 153

Saudi Arabia, 20–21
Schillhorn, Uwe, on risk scores, 92–93

Schwartz, Tony, on need to feel valued, 134
Scientific American, 30, 73
Seattle Times, 86
Sellers, Piers, 31–32
September 11, 2001 terrorist attacks, 49–50
The Seven Basic Plots (Christopher Booker), 29
"Seven Sacred Channels to the Mind," 141
Shah, Ashish V., 209–210
Silk, Kimberly, on using data to support decision-making, 70–71
Simmons, Annette, on listening, 141
Sinek, Simon, on creating meaning, 80
Sleeping Beauty story, 29
Social Impact Story Outline, 192–201
social influence, 152
The Sound of Music (film), 12–13
"stabilizing the patient," 134–135
Stalin, Josef, on tragedy vs. statistics, 191
Standing, Kelly, 161–163
Stanton, Andrew, on audiences, 175
Start With Why (Simon Sinek), 80
Star Wars (film), 30
Stein, Lisa, 30
Story (Robert McKee), *xx*
story(-ies)
    core components of, 5–6
    fact-based, 20–21
    plots of, 23–43
    trivial vs. profound, *xx–xxi*
    value of, vs. explaining your qualifications alone, *xvii–xviii*
    weaving data into your, 74–85
    see also specific headings, e.g.: collecting stories; telling your story
StoryPicture(s), 100–127
    best practices with, 125–127
    binding of key elements in, 119–122
    developing a story for, 122–124
    FEE as, 114–117

formulas as, 112–113
getting feedback on, 124
graphs as, 109–110
making your own, 117–125
pie charts as, 110–111
refining your, 125
selecting most important
    elements for, 118–119
Venn diagrams as, 104–109
Virtuous Cycle as, 101–104
storytelling
    with data, 65–88
    and networking, 177–180
    Three-Act Formula for, 11–13
    three rules of smart, 18–19
story vacuums, filling, 19–20
strategy, 6
stroke, 208–209
structure, 6, 11–13
    for complex topics, 95–96
    and telling your story, 155–156
Stryker Neurovascular, 208–209
Super Bowl, 30
Super Freakonomics (Harlan Coben
    and Stephen Dubner), 160
Switch (Chip and Dan Heath), 7
Syria, 20, 191
systems, 101–102
Systrom, Kevin, on Instagram app, 189
Szieszka, Jon, 47–49

Taylor, Robert, 209
Teerlink, Richard, 29
telling your story, 151–169
    examples of, 156–164
    and going from personal to
        persuasive, 161–164
    outline for, 165–167
    and story structure, 155–156
    and "tell me about yourself"
        question, 151–153
    and testing your story, 168–169
    and your audience, 154
"tell me about yourself" question,
    responding to the, 151–153
testing your story, 168–169
theme, 15–16, 33–34
Thompson, Lynn, 86–87

Three-Act Formula, 11–13, 53, 81–82,
    155, 192, *see also* Acknowledge–
    Inspire–Action (AIA) model
"Three Cs," 13
Three Little Pigs story, 47–49
Three Prep Questions (for data-based
    presentations), 74–76
time, losing track of, 23
Time magazine, 141
total overlap, 109
The True Story of the Three Little Pigs
    (Jon Szieszka), 47–49

"ugly first draft," 33
unfamiliar, comparing familiar to,
    92–94
Union Bank of Switzerland (UBS), 92
United Kingdom, 18, 20, 133
University Club of Chicago, 161
University of California, Santa
    Barbara, 187
University of Chicago, *xv–xviii*, 158
University of Toronto, 70
U.S. Bank, 56–64
US Department of Transportation, 85
US National Highway System, 85

vaccination, 19–20
vacuum cleaners, 32
Valence Health, 205–208
valued, feeling, 134
Venn diagrams, 104–109
Virtuous Cycle, 101–104
visuals, 99–100, *see also*
    StoryPicture(s)
Vonnegut, Kurt, 24–27, 33, 109

Wakefield, Andrew, 19–20
water filtration, 30–31
Weiner, Matthew, 15
Weinstein, Kevin, 205–208
Weiss, Alan, on effect of logic vs.
    emotion, 7
Wharton Business School, 213
"What Do You Do?" question,
    responding to, 177–181
Wheelan, Charles, on Central Limit
    Theorem, 94

whiteboards, 126
Winfrey, Oprah, 28
Wired, 87
words, vs. numbers, in data-based
    presentations, 78–80

World Series, 132–133
The World's Worst Pollution Problems
    (report), 30

ZS Associates, 53–55